Getting
Words to
Drive Action

Write
This
Way

Pat Butler & Charles Young

 www.trafford.com

North America & international
toll-free: 1 888 232 4444 (USA & Canada)
phone: 250 383 6864 ♦ fax: 812 355 4082

Foreword

You have sent your memo or document to your audience. You're worried they won't read it, or they'll read it but not respond the way you're hoping. Want to know why they might not?

You already know why. Why don't YOU read some things? When you do, is your heart in it? Do you wish the writer had done better for you?

Write This Way will guide you to that better place. By following the 4-step approach, you will produce writing more likely to be read and more likely to have the desired effect.

First objective: to get read. This means short, not long, with the WIIFM up front – What's In It For Me. "Okay, it's short; let me see what it's about." followed closely by, "I DO see what it's about; I'll keep reading." Or, "I'll hold on to this." You have **engaged** the reader.

Now, be kind to your readers by giving them what they want and need – no more, no less. Why not more? That means bigger – not good. Why not less? That means they won't have what's necessary – not good. So you **select** what to include, based on what they already know and what else they *need* to know.

Kindness only goes so far. Only the most motivated reader will stick with your writing if the material is not well **presented**. If you depend on their motivation, prepare to be disappointed. Think of a convenience store shelf display; think of your material.

Finally, you want to **perfect** your writing. Relax, we're speaking in relative terms. A less-than-professional impression will distract your reader, and could stir disrespect for the writer. Don't go there.

Come with us in *Write This Way*. We'll show you how.

Acknowledgements

This little book represents the culmination of several people's efforts over several years and I will take a moment to thank my friends and allies. I will share some background on how this book was born.

In my first job, I taught Physics at a high school—I have always enjoyed mechanical things, and reading or composing precise instructions. In a major career shift in the 1980's, I became an Instructional Technologist at a Canadian telecommunications giant, and found myself teaching courses in writing policies and procedures.

I then became a Performance Consultant, who (among other services) developed self-paced instruction to certify unionized manufacturing employees. Several clients then asked me to teach their employees some of my analysis and technical writing methods, so I developed a series of classroom-delivered courses.

Charles Young , a business partner at the time, is a performance-improvement zealot. He took a run at the content and the course became Writing for Action™. I have delivered the course to a multitude of clients in a variety of formats, including as a distance-education offering over the Internet—complete with personal, one-on-one coaching.

After I decided to self-publish this little book, its format and objectives have gone through a couple of metamorphoses. Charles became a co-author—while his never-ending quest for perfection can drive one to distraction, he is almost always right.

My sincere thanks to Stephen Butler for suggesting the title, to Lynda Myler for an early review, to Lesley Lucas, Alisha Wist, Jeffrey Butler, Mavis Young, and Karlye Butler for later reviews. Their willingness to go through the material with the reader's point-of-view top of mind has worked its magic.

Pat Butler, B.Sc., M.Ed.
Toronto, Ontario
May 2009

WRITE THIS WAY
Table of contents

1. Getting Started 1
  Why people write 1
    Why do you write? 1
    Why put it in writing? 1
    WIIFM principle 1
    Who is your audience? 2
    You are this book's audience 2
    Origin of this book 2
  How to succeed 2
    Do you care enough? 2
    It takes empathy and effort 3
    The right approach 3
  How to use this book 3
    Shop around 3
    Small changes, big differences 4
  An Overview of *Writing for Action*™ 4
    Your mission 4
    The four steps 4
    Engaging 5
    Selecting 5
    Presenting 6
    Perfecting 6
    Writing outside the box 6
    Whatever the medium 6
    Practice Exercises 6

2. Engaging 9
  Know your audience 9
    Who are they? 9
    What do I know about them? 9
    Doing the research 9
  Know your purpose 10
    What you want to accomplish 10
    Examples of purpose 10
  Connect with your audience 12
    Start with precision 12
    Keep them engaged 12

3. Selecting 13
  Estimating the minimum requirement 13
    Credit where credit is due 13
    Doing the math 13
    What if I *must* include something 13
    The stages of selecting 14
  1. Gathering information 14
    Available information 14
  2. Sorting into WWH (What, Why, How) 14
    Where does it fit 14
    Examples of WWH 14
    WHAT – the call to action 16
    WHAT – as email Subject 16
    WHY – the rationale 16
    WHY – the reader's role 17
    HOW – two categories 17
    HOW – as a process 17

Table of Contents

HOW – as a procedure 18

3. Filtering for relevance **18**

Making the cut 18

Setting the relevance bar...18

The relevance principle 19

Risks of irrelevant information 19

The WIIFM sensor 20

Feedback and testing 20

4. Presenting..**21**

Writing sentences..**21**

Write the way you speak 21

Structure on a page...**21**

Customize for your audience....................................21

Conventional sentences in paragraphs 21

Bullets..22

Bullet symbols 23

Numbering and lettering 23

Decimal page numbers...24

Instructions **25**

Numbered sentences 25

Recipe in a table 25

Recipes Checklist..26

Grouping aids retention 27

Tables **29**

Categorizing facts..29

Illustrating a process..29

Highlighting who is responsible 30

Guiding decision-making 31

Flowcharts..**32**

For specific audiences 32

Illustrations **32**

Add visual impact 32

Combinations...**33**

Purpose will guide you..33

Page layout **34**

Make each page appealing 34

Cues and units...34

One level up 34

Deriving cues...35

Guidelines for cues..36

One column with headings 37

Headings and the table of contents 37

Two columns 37

Pros & Cons of two columns.....................................39

Visible gridlines..40

Pros & Cons of visible gridlines 40

Finding information **41**

Table of Contents 41

Subject Index..42

Headers and Footers..42

Guideline for location...42

Perfecting comes later **43**

Details promote stardom 43

5. Perfecting...**44**

Active vs. passive..**44**

Comparisons 44

Why active is better 44

Table of Contents

Modifiers..**44**
   Use sparingly...44
Brevity **45**
   Help your reader understand................................45
   Watch sentence length 46
Consistent grammatical form **46**
   Make bullets match...46
Precision with words.......................................**47**
   Nouns rule 47
   Casting the sentence..48
   Consistent terminology 49
Dealing with he/she/they.................................**49**
   Be inclusive 49
Common grammatical errors............................**49**
Punctuation basics..**50**
   Commas 50
   Bullets..51
   Quotations 51
Text formatting...**52**
   Bold, italics, underline..52
   Capitalization and ALL CAPS 53
Font selection **54**
   Popular fonts 54
   Font types 55
   Font sizes 55
Proofreading **56**
   Another pair of eyes 56
   Checklist..56
6. Sharpening your skills.................................**57**
   Precision exercises...57
   Grammar exercises 59
Feedback **61**
Appendix **65**
   Recipe checklist...65
   Decision table checklist 65
   Report writing cue menu.......................................66
Slide Presentation Tips **67**
   Keep it simple 67
   What audiences find annoying..............................67
   Connecting with your audience.............................68
PowerPoint Basics **69**
   Start a new presentation.......................................69
   Create slides..70
   Apply a design template 71
   Customize the design 72
   Insert footers...75
   Preparing presentation notes...............................76
Creating a subject index **79**
   Create a concordance file.....................................79
   Mark the entries in your document 80
   Generate the index 80
   Update the index 81
Writing Planner **82**
Writing Checklist **83**
Subject Index **84**

1. Getting Started

Why people write

Why do <u>you</u> write?

If you write to keep in touch with others, to reach out and share your news and views, then *just do it!*

But, if you write to influence what your readers think, how they feel, and what they do, then you need to:

✓ engage them

✓ equip them

✓ guide them.

Why put it in writing?

Let's say you could speak directly to your audience. Would you bother to write? Should you bother to write?

Yes and yes. Because …

○ there's only so much people will remember. If you are speaking to them—at a meeting for example—also give them a handout summarizing your message. Then you can concentrate on *engaging* them aloud, knowing that you have put in their hands the information they will need *after* the meeting.

○ you can organize the information exactly the way the user will need it when the time comes. So when the time comes to take action, the reader will be able to quickly find and easily follow your instructions. Call it just-in-time information.

Also, there are many situations when you cannot speak to your audience because it would be too impractical. They may be spread across the company, across the city, or across the world.

This book will help you write emails and letters, as well as instructions, meeting minutes, reports, and technical manuals.

WIIFM principle

You pick up the newspaper or visit a website. You scan the headings. You read some articles, you skip a bunch. You and millions of readers routinely apply the **What's In It For Me** principle.

Is it interesting? Will I learn something? Is this worth my limited time? WIIFM?

You scan your email inbox. Is this important? Do I care? Who wants to know? How does this affect me? WIIFM?

1. Getting Started

Is this bad behaviour?

No. It's human nature, and it's the only practical way to handle all the written information that exists in the world.

Who is your audience?

Are they close family and best friends who love you and will read everything you write regardless?

Or are they people with WIIFMs?

So, you have two choices when you write:

1. Assume your audience wants to think, feel, and act like you do so you can just express yourself.
2. Don't assume, and pay close attention to the WIIFMs.

You are this book's audience

We have paid close attention to your WIIFM.

We want you to keep using this book because you want to influence what people think, how they feel, and what they do.

This book was written for you, and we want you to use this book to achieve your goals.

Then you'll be glad you used it. You will keep it nearby as a quick-reference. And you will tell others about it so they will also benefit from using our little book. They start achieving their goals, and their readers benefit, too.

Wow! Call it a culture of effective writing sweeping the world.

Origin of this book

Over several decades, the authors have provided consulting and technical writing services to large and small organizations in North America. They developed a series of courses entitled "Writing for Action" for clients seeking to improve their employees' business writing skills.

The time has come to share this *Writing for Action*™ methodology with a global audience.

How to succeed

Do you care enough?

Hallmark cards wants us to "… care enough to send the very best"—arguably the most enduring slogan in history.

A. Writers may not care enough about their purpose, so they don't send their very best.
B. Writers may in fact be sending their very best, but it's not as good as it could be.
C. Writers may not know what the very best looks like.

1. Getting Started

We can't help you with A. We will help you with B and C.

It takes empathy and effort

Empathy is about putting yourself in your readers' shoes—those shoes your readers will be wearing when they read your writing.

Their "shoes" are their interests, diligence, values, ability, knowledge, patience, and trust.

If what you write is …

- too long—they may not bother reading it
- too complicated—they may not understand it
- too technical—they may make mistakes when trying to apply it
- too disorganized—they may give up.

If your writing does not have enough of the right stuff, in the right order, in the right words, they may put it aside (possibly forever).

The successful writer empathizes and makes the effort to engage, equip, and guide the reader. They offer writing that is the *quickest* to grasp, *easiest* to follow, *surest* to work.

The right approach

Writing for Action™ proposes four stages:

1 Engaging   2 Selecting   3 Presenting   4 Perfecting

When you *engage* your audience with empathy and purpose, they are encouraged to pay attention.

When you *select* content (explaining what they need to know and do), they appreciate your omission of the unnecessary.

When you *present* information in bite-sized chunks in the right order, they understand more easily.

When you *perfect* your writing with clear expression and consistent terms, in concise form with precise language, your audience is empowered to act.

When you do the above, you are on your way to being recognized as a "great communicator," maybe even a star!

How to use this book

Shop around

As a writer, you may already be doing some of what this book teaches. You have what is called "unconscious competence," that is, you are writing pretty well without knowing it.

1. Getting Started

In that case, shop around the table of contents with your WIIFM basket. See something you like? Enjoy. Something seems to be unexplained? Check earlier topics.

"Write This Way" is not a textbook. It certainly makes sense going from front to back, but who says that will work best for you? Think of it as a Guidebook or maybe a buffet. You can eat dessert first and the salad last, and still have a healthy meal.

"Write This Way" is a practical guide to get you where you want to go. Feel free to cherry-pick and have fun!

Small changes, big differences

If you've got writing to do, don't put off applying the principles you learn here until you've read and digested the whole book.

Have faith that *small* improvements in your output (what you write) can make a *big* difference in the outcome (what readers do). Your writing may already be at the 5'11" mark, and the bar is at 6'. You've been knocking off the bar, but one more inch will get you over!

The more frequently you apply the principles of *Writing for Action*™, the more fluent you become in thinking and writing effectively. Fluency makes you quicker and clearer, so don't wait until you have to write a major report to exercise your writing. Do it now and do it often.

An Overview of *Writing for Action*™

Your mission

Your mission is to move your audience to *take action* by influencing what they think, how they feel, and what they do.

The four steps

This step...	Involves...	And is covered in...
Engaging	Your audience Your purpose	Chapter 2
Selecting	What they need to know What they need to do	Chapter 3
Presenting	Bite-sized chunks Suitable structures	Chapter 4
Perfecting	Being clear Being consistent Being concise Being precise	Chapter 5

1. Getting Started

Engaging

In *engaging* your audience you must know them as well as you know your purpose. What are they like? What are their beliefs and values? In their view of the world, or of your purpose in particular, where are they "coming from"? Knowing who they are is the first step to influencing them.

Engaging your audience in your writing goes beyond the actual words you use. The phenomenon of non-verbal communications applies partly to writing and reading as it does to speaking and hearing. In Albert Mehrabian's landmark communications studies on feelings and attitudes, he proposed the 7%-38%-55% Rule. For the meaning of the message in face-to-face communications, words account for 7%, tone of voice accounts for 38%, and body language accounts for 55%. In other words, the receiver gets most of the meaning from non-verbal content.

In writing, there is no body language, but there most definitely is *tone*. If the reader perceives warmth, friendliness, respect, consideration, or other positive qualities in the *tone* of your writing, then the likeability factor that Mehrabian studied will be in your favour. People pay more attention to communicators they like.

Selecting

In *selecting* the right content, you need to tell readers:

- **W**hat to do
- **W**hy they should do it
- **H**ow to do it.

Since readers don't want to waste their time, they expect the author to tell them:

- **W**hat to do
- **W**hy they should do it
- **H**ow to do it.

What a coincidence!

Selecting content for your writing comes down to the difference between what the reader needs to know about what, why, how (**WWH**) and what they already know.

To illustrate this mathematically:

Minimum content you need to provide = WWH required – WWH already known.

Content you provide is not restricted to the difference, but represents the minimum. You will often provide more in order to provide sufficient context and continuity. An individual reader can always skip content he or she already knows.

Presenting

In *presenting* your content, you will look at how to organize and present information in bite-sized chunks with respect to:

- content (what reader needs to know)
- direction (what reader needs to do)
- hierarchy and sequence
- cues and units
- visual weights and elements.

Perfecting

In *perfecting* your work, you will

- write clearly so readers can follow easily
- keep it brief so they don't stop and do something else
- use terms they know so they are not misled or perplexed
- use precise language so they get it right the first time.

Writing outside the box

While the *Writing for Action*™ methodology is not about creative writing, you can be creative in your business or technical writing. It takes imagination to make a dull subject interesting. Interesting writing helps to engage readers.

Your focus is on giving readers information that will drive action, but their action will depend on what they think and how they feel. A creative spirit will help you to put yourself in the mind of the reader. When you begin to think and feel like one of them, you can see your own writing as they might.

If they think you are assuming too much or are not very helpful, or that you got it wrong, they will pay scant attention to what you have to say. If they don't feel like doing what you ask, they may not!

Whatever the medium

Whether you use Word, PowerPoint, Outlook, webmail, pen and paper, or flip chart and markers to produce memos, paper documents, pdf files, emails, web pages, or slide presentations, the principles of *Writing for Action*™ apply.

Practice Exercises

Your own job or project offers excellent practice opportunities. Colleagues, even family members and friends, can review and

1. Getting Started

give feedback. If you would like to practice with other material, we've provided practice exercises under **Sharpening your skills**.

The *before* scenarios are included on the enclosed CD, in case you want to edit the actual text. The *after* scenarios are in "Write This Way" for easy comparison. Unlike mathematics with one right answer, writing has a variety of good answers, only one of which is shown.

2. Engaging

Know your audience

Who are they?

Your audience may be one person or thousands of people, for example:

- Your manager or supervisor
- Co-workers in your department
- Potential clients
- A dissatisfied customer
- The president of a company you are complaining to
- Your lawyer or accountant
- Product users

What do I know about them?

Ask yourself:

- What do they know about this subject?
- How do they feel about the issue?
- How many pages will they read, regardless of how well written?
- What is their general disposition to reading and their reading ability?
- How familiar are they with technical terms?

Add questions that apply to your audience and your situation.

The more you know, the better you can customize your writing and the more influence you will have with your audience. Ask questions. Time spent doing research will have enormous payoff.

Doing the research

To get a handle on ...	check out ...
What they already know How they feel about the issue	Their background and experience The history of and issues surrounding the subject The current "buzz" on the subject, good and bad
Maximum number of pages	How time pressured they usually are

2. Engaging

To get a handle on ...	check out ...
	How much other reading material they get
Reading ability and general disposition to reading	Level of education Eyesight limitations Work environment conditions How much reading they typically do
Familiarity with technical language	Types of work performed Typical experience levels Levels of training

Know your purpose

What you want to accomplish

You have a purpose for writing. You want readers to take action: behave differently, agree with you, do something they might not otherwise do.

The outcome you seek may be immediate or in the future. It may be covert (changed values, beliefs that lead to changed behaviour later), or it may be overt (visible action now).

If you seek compliance to a policy, you may feel that you don't need to change hearts—you've got the authority and you will request compliance.

If you seek a more reliable and enduring change in attitude and behaviour, then you will want to change hearts too. You will work harder in your writing to engage the audience in your mission.

Examples of purpose

I want the reader to ...	Example
Take action *now*	• *Decide to hire me* • *Enter a different code into a computer form* • *Play a role in a process* • *Send me a new widget that works* • *Use the farthest parking spaces to leave the nearest for customers* • *Follow a new policy* • *Attend a meeting prepared (having read the agenda)*

2. Engaging

I want the reader to ...	Example
	• *Share information with others (e.g., junior staff)* • *Carry out responsibilities I am assigning*
Take action in the *future*	• *Use sales or production figures when required* • *Respond correctly in an emergency* • *Adhere to a policy being implemented two months from today*
Make a decision	• *Approve my plan or budget* • *Select one of the options presented* • *Propose a launch date for the new product* • *Accept a recommendation*
Follow instructions	• *Complete and submit the attached form* • *Perform a task following the new procedure* • *Use new software* • *Use the colour-coded recycling bins correctly*
Provide input	• *Review the proposed plan and give feedback* • *Assess the situation and make recommendations* • *Suggest ways to fix a problem*
Support me	• *Agree with my recommendation and support it in the meeting* • *Vote for me* • *Recommend my services to others*
Be motivated	• *Participate enthusiastically in the campaign* • *Greet and serve customers warmly* • *Promote the new product at every opportunity*

2. Engaging

Connect with your audience

Start with precision

When you know your audience and your purpose, your writing can then be purposeful.

Your cover letter, memo, or the first sentence of your document will reflect:

- who the audience is (because it's addressed to them)
- why they are being engaged
- what's in it for them (their WIIFMs – personal, professional, communal, global, etc.), whether plainly stated or subtly referenced.

Keep them engaged

To keep them engaged, try to be brief. This means being strict on what to leave out. This can be the hardest part for a knowledgeable writer who cares a lot about the subject.

A helpful rule is, "When in doubt, leave it out." Yes, you take a chance on leaving out information. At the same time, you reduce the risk that the amount of text will overwhelm the reader. This is covered in **Selecting**.

3. Selecting

Estimating the minimum requirement

Credit where credit is due

Imagine you are preparing to teach a friend how to do something that you are pretty good at.

Fill in the blank: "I am teaching X how to _____" (putt a golf ball, cook dinner, hit a baseball, browse the Internet, paint a room, etc.).

Before starting to teach, you would have an idea (or ask questions to find out), what experience or knowledge your friend already has on the subject. You wouldn't assume he has done nothing or knows nothing. You wouldn't want to bore him, waste his time, or worse, insult him by starting from scratch.

Doing the math

For people to take *action*, they'll need to know what you are asking them to do, why they should do it, and know how to do it. We refer to these as the What, Why, How or WWH.

Quite likely, your audience already has some of the WWH in their background or from their current roles. As stated earlier:

> Minimum content you need to provide = WWH required – WWH already known.

That's the minimum. You will usually provide a bit more for context and continuity. Sometimes it's hard to connect the dots when you're not sure what the picture is. So, you'll need to paint enough of the picture so readers can see where you are going.

The larger your audience, the more variable their WWH can be. In **Presenting**, you will see how to present content so the reader can readily browse, skip over what they know, and find what they need. Think buffet.

What if I *must* include something

Yes, we are not the supreme boss of all that we do. Sometimes we must include content that does not meet our criteria for inclusion. This is the cool part of **Presenting**. The right structure will make it easy for readers to navigate the content and to quickly find what *they* need.

The stages of selecting

There are 3 stages in selecting content:

1. Gathering information
2. Sorting into WWH
3. Filtering for relevance

1. Gathering information

Available information

In the gathering stage, you scout the environment for available information. You don't need to be very strict:

- pages of a manual
- an article
- Wikipedia entry
- comments from an expert
- a couple of Google hits
- what your boss wants
- the latest string of emails
- your views on the subject, etc.

2. Sorting into WWH (What, Why, How)

Where does it fit

The framework for content is WWH:

What is the issue? What are you proposing? What are you asking me to do? This is the call to *action*.

Why does this matter? Why should I care? Why are you asking *me*? This is the *rationale*.

How do I do this thing you are asking? How will I tell when I'm doing it right? This is the *how-to*.

If a bank is rolling out a new on-line staff travel expense form, the email announcement will offer WHAT (the form you must submit for travel expenses), WHY (information required for approval and audit), and HOW (instructions to complete and submit).

Examples of WWH

Imagine you have been asked to give people directions to get things done. Locate the WWH as you read through each of these examples.

3. Selecting

Example 1

The dog needs to be walked.

To a visiting child: *"Would you take Skippy out for a walk? He's got to go and he needs the exercise. Please use the leash, go to the park, and take the plastic bags."*

Example 2

The family needs a tent.

To a 20 year-old: *"Look for a tent that holds 6 people and has a window on every side. There are only 4 of us but I know we'll love the extra room and the extra light. The Eurotrip store has the best selection and prices. Try to stay under $250. Call me on my cellphone if you're not sure which to buy.*

Example 3

A meeting needs to be arranged.

To your assistant: *"Please arrange a meeting for <date, time> with <persons>. We need to move this project forward now and these are the decision-makers. Send them an email proposing that date and time. If any cannot make it, propose <date, time> as a alternate. When the meeting is confirmed, please book a room and order refreshments.*

Example 4

The new vacation policy is to be communicated.

To your assistant: *"Please draft a memo to all employees on the new vacation policy. They need to know by the middle of January so we can have the schedule completed by the end of February. We'll distribute as an email message and refer to the HR Policy Manual being updated shortly.*

Example 5

A Financial Planner writes to a client on preparing for their meeting.

"We will be looking at your income from all sources and all investments, registered and non-registered, plus life insurance. This will enable us to discuss all the angles and prepare a comprehensive plan right through to retirement and post-retirement. List all of your income and all of your investments on a sheet of paper, or bring all of your statements for the past 3 months and your last CRA Notice of Assessment."

3. Selecting

WHAT – the call to action

"What this is about" is the first thing the audience needs to know, and wants to know. It could be:

- the situation, problem, issue, or need that requires their attention
- the outcome or decision that deserves their support
- the action they need to take and when
- the answers to their questions in preparation for action.

You are writing to elicit a response of some kind from each member of your audience. This is the call to action.

You may be thinking, "But I want to tell my story first, to draw them in, to pique their interest, to motivate them BEFORE I say what I'm asking them to do." That's a fair proposition for creative writing and literary journalism.

In "Write This Way," we're dealing with a business audience. Business audiences tend to have limited time for reading. So, when they approach their Inbox or In-basket, they quickly choose what to read and what to skip. If you don't tell them what you are writing about up front, you risk being skipped.

WHAT – as email Subject

Have you ever received an email whose Subject bears little or no connection to its content? This is likely because this email is part of an ongoing discussion, or thread, and later writers have not taken trouble to edit the Subject inserted by the originator.

Typically, the Subject begins to disconnect from the discussion at about the 3rd Reply/All. Because the email Subject is often the WHAT of the dialogue, the original WHAT soon becomes meaningless.

With every Reply/All, you have the opportunity to update the Subject. While there is the risk of "changing the subject," there is often greater risk in a subject that is no longer relevant to the developing discussion. The risk escalates as the audience grows; new persons included may be misled by the original Subject.

WHY – the rationale

Now that you've got their momentary attention, tell them WHY—why they should care, why this is important, what will happen if …. Give them the WIIFM. You may feel there isn't much of a WIIFM. That's life—give them what you've got.

3. Selecting

Examples

- *I really hope you can attend the meeting because others need to hear your insights on this problem.*
- *The new policy has been developed in order that staff in the two merged departments all enjoy the same benefits.*
- *I know you are not planning to buy a house for another six months, but I want to keep you informed of current prices in your target area.*

WHY – the reader's role

In some situations, the reader is the middleman between the person who started the process and the person who will complete it. Readers will better understand the situation and their role if they know where they fit. The context you provide will make their contribution clearer and could motivate them to hold up their end of the bargain.

Example

You will soon be receiving Client Satisfaction Questionnaires from across the country. You will co-ordinate information between the clients and the Statistics Department.

HOW – two categories

Required information can be a few facts, several concepts, or a detailed exposition. The action items can require a few steps or many. As you gather how-to information, you may find it fits into two separate categories:

- Process – how stages happen over time
- Procedure – what to do

HOW – as a process

A major benefit of describing a process is that people involved each see where they fit from beginning to end, and how their individual actions relate to one another's and contribute to the end product.

Example

To a realtor's house-buying client:

"Whenever you see a newspaper or website listing for a house you are interested in viewing, please call me. I will be delighted to set up a time for us to view the house together. That way, the listing realtor will not be confused and think you are a new prospect. I will be ready to help you decide whether to make an offer."

3. Selecting

HOW – as a procedure

A major benefit of a procedure is that the people involved can read and act with immediacy and certainty. A well-written procedure does not rely on the reader's memory, intuition, analytical ability, or abundant knowledge. It spells out what to do so the reader gets it right the first time and every time.

Example

To a realtor's house-selling client:

"To prepare your house to be listed, do the following:

1. *Set up an appointment with our Staging Consultant to develop a plan to present your house for maximum appeal.*
2. *Carry out all the necessary painting and repairs as written in the plan.*
3. *Remove clutter by taking items to temporary storage.*
4. *Invite the Consultant for final staging (table-setting, fresh flowers, etc.)*
5. *Arrange the photography session with me."*

3. Filtering for relevance

Making the cut

Only talented athletes make the cut to be on the team. Similarly, only the information that counts makes the cut to your finished product. Without filtering, your writing will end up bigger than it needs to be. Size matters—the smaller the better. The primary filter is *relevance*.

Setting the relevance bar

Imagine that you are driving alone, in the rain, at night, on the deserted streets of an unfamiliar city. A warning light on the dashboard of your rental car starts to flash. You pull over and reach in the glove compartment for the Owner's Guide.

The Owner's Guide has many sections and pages. You have trouble finding the *relevant* information. It may be nothing serious, but there might be something you have to do to continue safely. You are frustrated and worried.

The authors of the manual have set the bar low. It has lots of interesting narrative that drivers will never read, and it has information on the warning light. First, you have to find that bit. Then you hope that bit will tell you clearly what's going on what you need to do.

If you expect your readers to take a leisurely approach and read whatever comes across their desk or screen, then you can set the bar low. If you have to compete for their attention and action, then you will want to raise the bar.

The relevance principle

Relevance is the measure of information's value to your *purpose* and to your readers' *needs*. Your document should be as long as it has to be, and not one line more.

At the gathering stage, you can be inclusive. At the filtering stage, your mantra becomes, "When in doubt, leave it out."

Say to yourself, "If I left this section (fact, paragraph, data, etc.) out, the reader would:

- not believe me
- not understand me
- not want to do the right thing
- not know why it makes a difference
- not know how to do it."

At least one of these statements must be true for a piece of content to make the cut to your final document.

Risks of irrelevant information

Low-relevance content will make your writing longer—2 pages instead of 1 page, 1 page instead of 6 bullet points, 100 pages instead of 50. Be ruthless in leaving out nice-to-know, interesting, or historical information that matters a lot to some people, but not enough to your audience and your purpose.

A common perception among readers is that length = time = difficulty. Who's got time? Who wants a difficult time?

If you include irrelevant content, readers may:

- misunderstand your purpose
- misinterpret the instructions
- become confused
- get frustrated
- feel inadequate if terminology is beyond them
- fail to act in a timely manner
- criticize you or your purpose.

Example

A Computer User Guide for bank branch staff explains how the software was customized for this bank. This may be relevant to IT support staff, but is likely irrelevant to users.

3. Selecting

The WIIFM sensor

Readers will typically spend less time perusing your writing than you would like. What they pay attention to will depend on its relevance. Without conscious effort, their WIIFM sensor scans headings and text and immediately sends relevance signals. Too low and it's a skip. When the sensor lights up, there's something here for *me* and I pause to read.

Feedback and testing

Having others read your writing is invaluable. There will be flaws you missed and assumptions you unknowingly made. Don't rely on the experts only. The best test will be members of your audience. This is where the "When in doubt, leave it out" gets validated. If they "get it" and can "do it," then you made the right decisions. If you did the opposite and left "maybe" content in, then you won't know if readers could have done without it.

This is not an argument for blunt, dry, humourless writing. The principle is to make every bit of content count. Engaging your audience is important. Do it with economy and with elegance, not with excess.

Excess slows access.

4. Presenting

Writing sentences

Write the way you speak

Think of a learned acquaintance (perhaps a lawyer, professor, accountant, or engineer) and try to recall a conversation you shared. When this person spoke to you about his or her professional opinion, did you understand right away or did you need to ask for clarification? It is likely the spoken words and sentence structures were clear to you. Excellent!

Now, picture that person conveying the professional opinion in *writing*. Wouldn't it be wonderful if the written words had the same level of clarity as the spoken words? Sadly, this is rarely the case. Some very bright, successful business managers and professionals feel the need to write in a complicated, verbally dense style—possibly because they subconsciously feel the need to show how smart they are! They may be trying to emulate colleagues or use the writing technique employed during their academic studies.

Truth is— truly smart people use simple, straightforward sentences when they speak *and write*.

You will learn about sentence structure in **Perfecting** and then practice making improvements in **Sharpening your skills**.

Structure on a page

Customize for your audience

Information needs to be presented in bite-sized chunks in a structure customized for the audience. This chapter covers a variety of options you can use.

- If there are 5 points to make, you can use 5 paragraphs for lawyers and 5 bullet points for office staff.

- If you are instructing on software, you can use text steps #1-5 for experienced users and screen exhibits #1-5 for new users.

- If you are communicating a new policy, you can use a flowchart for engineering staff and a table for administrative staff.

Conventional sentences in paragraphs

A paragraph should cover one idea or point. Short paragraphs with a few sentences are generally better than long paragraphs.

4. Presenting

Similarly, short sentences are generally better than long sentences with multiple clauses. Have you read any legal documents lately?

Example of legal document

The application was opposed by the plaintiff in this proceeding ("XY Capital"), in its capacity as agent for a group of secured lenders (collectively, with XY Capital, the "Secured Lenders") who brought a cross-application for the appointment of a receiver.

It takes time to decode complex writing.

Example after Writing for Action

The plaintiff is XY Capital. They are acting as agent for a group of secured lenders (including XY Capital itself), hereafter referred to as the "Secured Lenders." The plaintiff opposed the application and brought a cross-application for the appointment of a receiver.

Bullets

When should you use bullets? Use them whenever you have a list of some kind. Sometimes, you'll write a bunch of sentences and not notice the list within. A reviewer may see it first. After you've done a few conversions, you'll begin to see the bullets sooner. Three bullets are easier to follow than three sentences in a paragraph.

Example 1

Before: *For the picnic, we need to buy disposable dishes, disposable cutlery, paper napkins, disposable cups, drinks, and a bag of ice.*

After: *For the picnic, we need to buy:*

- *disposable dishes*
- *disposable cutlery*
- *paper napkins*
- *disposable cups*
- *drinks*
- *bag of ice.*

If you were in charge of buying, which form would you find more helpful?

Think of bullets as commas separating the listed items (of course, in the above example you do not really need a comma before "disposable dishes") and then end the sentence with a period (after "ice"). If you follow this convention, you will avoid the visual clutter that would occur if you had a comma after *every* item. Simple is better.

Example 2

Before: *Replace the filter on the Filler when the soap flakes are lumpy, it takes more than 20 seconds to fill a box, or a pile of soap flakes forms on the floor.*

After: *Replace the filter on the Filler when any one of these occurs:*

- *The soap flakes are lumpy.*
- *It takes more than 20 seconds to fill a box.*
- *A pile of soap flakes forms on the floor.*

Note the use of periods at the end of each item, because each item in the list is a complete sentence.

Bullet symbols

Bullet symbols can be round dots, square dots, circles, boxes, check marks, arrows, and all manner of Wingdings. Use the same symbol for all the items within a list. Within a single document, feel free to use a variety of bullet symbols to indicate a type of content.

- The dot (not a period!) is probably the most common bullet symbol. In MS Word and Mac, you can use font size to make the dot bigger, independent of the text font.
- ✓ If you are listing product features or accomplishments, you could use checkmarks.
- ❑ If you are listing criteria to be met or checklist items, you could use a box (a shadow box in this case).

Pick the 2 or 3 symbols for your document, then stop playing around. More than 3 could make the reader dizzy. Your choice may be restricted by the culture of your business.

Numbering and lettering

Numbers and letters are forms of bullets that indicate the items are sequential.

Example 1

A procedure for winterizing a cottage washer could be written :

1. *With the water hoses turned OFF, pour 2 litres of antifreeze into the washer.*
2. *Run a short wash for 5 minutes.*
3. *When you hear liquid being drained, turn the washer OFF.*

4. Presenting

Whether to indent (as shown) or not is your call. If the content has no sequence, do *not* use numbers or letters.

Letters are often the next level in a sequence.

Example 2

Thus, if step 2 shown above had 3 sub-steps, it would appear as:

2   *Run a short wash for 5 minutes.*

     a.   *With no clothes inside, close the washer door.*

     b.   *Turn the knob to SHORT WASH.*

     c.   *To start the washer, pull the knob towards you.*

This is a popular hierarchy of numbers and letters:

I.   Roman numeral one.

II.   Roman numeral two.

    A.   First capital letter

    B.   Second capital letter

      1.   Arabic number one

      2.   Arabic number two

        a.   First lowercase letter

        b.   Second lowercase letter

          i.   First lowercase roman

          ii.   Second lowercase roman

Notice the alternating of letters and numbers.

In highly complex documents without sequences, numbers and letters may also be used for ease of reference. If you will be referring to particular items, e.g., "Objective 3" or "Clause C", the number or letter quickly singles out what you are talking about.

Decimal page numbers

You may wish to use decimal page numbers to connect with chapters, as this Guidebook does. In addition to ease of referencing, there is convenience of updating.

Example

When you insert additional content into Chapter 3 after page 3-11, you only need to re-issue from page 3-12 to the end of the Chapter. Without decimal numbering you would have to reissue pages to the end of the whole document!

Instructions

Numbered sentences

Using a conventional structure, you can just tell readers what to do. It might seem authoritarian, but if readers don't know how to do something, they want straightforward instructions. After you present the WHAT and the WHY, *tell* them HOW.

This kind of straight talk can be called a recipe.

Example

How to hand-wash a delicate wool sweater:

1. *Pour 2 capfuls of Gentle Care detergent into wash basin.*

2. *Add 4 litres of cold water.*

3. *Place the sweater to soak in the sudsy water for 3 minutes.*

4. *Squeeze the sudsy water out of the sweater.* **Do not wring!** *This could permanently distort the sweater.*

5. *Rinse the sweater in cold water and squeeze out the excess. Rinse twice.*

6. *Lay the sweater flat on a bath towel.*

7. *Roll up together and press.*

8. *If necessary, repeat with another dry towel.*

9. *Lay the sweater flat and shape it on a drying rack or a dry towel.*

10. *Allow to dry completely.*

Recipe in a table

A recipe placed into a table makes it easy for the reader to keep track of progress.

Think back to the last time you followed a relatively complicated recipe in a cookbook. After carrying out each step, you probably had to *re-read* the procedure paragraph to find what to do next. If all cooks wrote cookbook recipes in tables as shown below, their readers would be *thrilled* to skip the re-reading!

4. Presenting

Example

Washing clothes in an automatic washer

STEP	ACTION
1	*Sort the dirty clothes into light and dark colours.*
2	*Pour the recommended amount of detergent into the washer.* *IMPORTANT: Use a measuring cup.*
3	*Place the light-coloured clothes in the washer, loosely and evenly around the whole tub.* *NOTE: Do not compress the clothes to get them all in—you may need to do a second load.*
4	*Select [HOT WASH / COLD RINSE] and start the washer.* *Result: Water will start entering the tub.* *NOTE: The wash cycle will take approximately 20 minutes.*
5	*When the wash cycle is complete:* • *move the clothes into the plastic laundry basket* • *place in dryer or hang to dry.*
6	*Repeat Steps 3 to 5 for dark-coloured clothes, selecting [COLD WASH / COLD RINSE].*

Recipes Checklist

Several features of this example can be summarized into a Recipes Checklist:

❑ Name the task.

❑ Speak to the reader using action verbs (e.g. Place, Press).

❑ Use "NOTE:" to separate additional information from the action.

❑ Use "Result:" to separate the result from the action.

❑ If the step contains several items, list with bullet points.

❑ Use a consistent format to represent item in the same class (e.g. fields on a screen, parts of equipment)

❑ Place "if" condition at the beginning of a step.

4. Presenting

 Highlight only critical words with bold, italics, underline, or all capitals. Be consistent.

☐ Make each step small enough so the reader is able to do it without having to re-read it.

Grouping aids retention

We memorize telephone numbers and our social insurance number in groups of digits. Similarly, readers find it easy to grasp and follow information in bite-size chunks. Memory research shows that short-term memory can only hold five to nine items at a time.

Example

The 29 steps required to move to a new house have been grouped into fewer than 9 steps per task.

1. Sell your current house

    a. Select a real estate agent

    b. Decide the asking price

    c. Using the services of a Staging Consultant, prepare the house for sale

    d. Welcome potential buyers to viewings

    e. Vacate the premises during Open Houses

    f. Respond to offers

    g. Reach agreement with a buyer and set closing date

2. Purchase a new house

    a. Select a real estate agent in a target neighbourhood

    b. Decide the price range you can afford

    c. Explore websites, newspaper advertisements, and target neighbourhoods

    d. Visit Open Houses

    e. Select a house that meets your criteria

    f. With your agent, prepare an offer

    g. Negotiate with seller

    h. When your offer is accepted, present certified cheque as deposit

4. Presenting

3. Prepare for moving day

    a.   Decide on moving day

    b.   Hire a moving company

    c.   Locate packing materials (when possible, use recycled materials)

    d.   Declutter by holding a garage sale and sending items to a charity

    e.   Starting with items not needed on a daily basis, pack and clearly label portable items

    f.   Finish packing everything being moved, with clear labelling

4. Move

    a.   At your old house, direct traffic as the movers place your packed items and unwrapped furniture and appliances in the truck

    b.   Treat your family to a restaurant meal

    c.   Drive to your new house

    d.   Direct traffic as the movers place your packed items and unwrapped furniture and appliances in the new house

    e.   Unpack essential items to get you through the first (beds, toothbrushes, cereal for breakfast)

    f.   Go to sleep

    g.   Start unpacking and arranging furniture and belongings in your new house

    h.   Celebrate!

4. Presenting

Tables

Categorizing facts

When you need to categorize related facts or options, a table is easy to read and can summarize a lot of information. The reader can easily compare options.

Example – two column table

Type of accommodation	Benefits to occupant
Rental apartment or duplex	• One storey is convenient • Short-term lease allows flexibility
Rental townhouse	• Two storeys provides extra space • Short-term lease allows flexibility
Condominium	• One storey is convenient • Ownership builds equity
Multi-storey house	• Several storeys provide extra space • Ownership builds equity

Illustrating a process

In **Selecting** this example of a process was given.

To a realtor's house-buying client: *"Whenever you see a newspaper or website listing for a house you are interested in viewing, please call me. I will be delighted to set up a time for us to view the house together. That way, the listing realtor will not be confused and think you are a new prospect. I will be ready to help you decide whether to make an offer."*

Now we will illustrate a way to present this process in a table with two columns. Notice that the verbs are in the present tense (e.g. locate, contact)

Example 1

Visiting a property for sale

Stage	Description
1	Buyers locate a property which they would like to visit
2	Buyers contact their real estate agent by phone or email to request a viewing
3	Agent sets up appointment for viewing by contacting the listing realtor

4. Presenting

Stage	Description
4	*Listing realtor sets up appointment for viewing by contacting the sellers*
5	*Sellers vacate the property*
6	*Buyers and agent visit the property*

Example 2

Producing home-grown tomatoes

Stage	Description
1	*Nursery grows tomato seedlings in hothouse*
2	*When local weather is frost-free, gardener buys seedlings at nursery outlet*
3	*Gardener plants seedlings in garden, then feeds and waters plants as they grow*
4	*As green tomatoes get heavy, gardener ties each plant to wooden stake for support*
5	*As tomatoes turn red, gardener harvests mature tomatoes amid family applause*

Highlighting who is responsible

As many processes involve multiple people, you can use a third column to break out who is responsible for each stage.

Example

The Stages of Professional Development at JKL Company

Stage		Responsibility	Actions
1	*Choose course*	*Employee*	• *decides which skills to upgrade* • *chooses appropriate external course* • *discusses plan with supervisor*
2	*Approve course*	*Supervisor*	• *approves the course per guidelines* • *notifies human resources*
3	*Submit form*	*Human Resources Department*	• *updates employee record to show course enrolment* • *sends employee reimbursement form*
4	*Complete course*	*Employee*	• *registers and pays for course* • *completes course* • *shows course certificate to*

4. Presenting

Stage	Responsibility	Actions
		supervisor
		• obtains supervisor's signature on reimbursement form
		• sends reimbursement form to human resources dept.
5	Reimburse employee	Human Resources Department	• updates employee record to show course completed
			• requests reimbursement cheque for employee

Guiding decision-making

When there are multiple conditions leading to different outcomes, a decision table is the wise choice. If read aloud, each option will read through as a complete, grammatically correct sentence.

Example 1

Attention sales clerks: The customer must be 19 years or older to legally buy cigarettes.

IF the customer appears to be ...	AND ...	proving age to be ...	THEN...
at least 25 years old	⟶	⟶	Make the sale
less than 25 years old	shows: • a driver's license • a passport, or • another government-issued photo ID	19 or more years	
		less than 19 years	Refuse to sell
	does <u>not</u> show a government-issued photo ID		

Example 2

Before:

If it is a white form, send it to the A Department. Send it to the B department if it is blue and signed. If it is blue and not signed, send it to the C Department.

After:

If the form colour is ...	AND it is ...	THEN send it to ...
White	⟶	A Dept
Blue	signed	B Dept
	not signed	C Dept

Flowcharts

For specific audiences

Flowcharts can be drawn for processes and procedures. They help the reader to visualize happens and/or to take action.

Just as a person is born either right or left-handed, it can be said that a person is born either liking or disliking reading flowcharts. Before taking the trouble to design one, decide whether your readers will find it helpful or confusing. People in technical professions, like engineering or computer science, often like flowcharts.

Example

How to sell your house

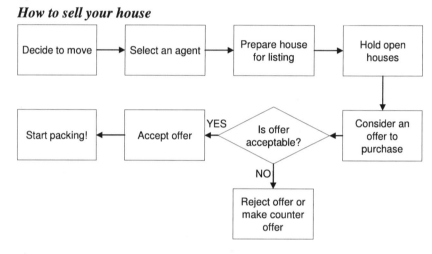

Illustrations

Add visual impact

Illustrations follow the principle that "a picture is worth a thousand words."

Example: Step 9 of "How to hand-wash a delicate wool sweater"

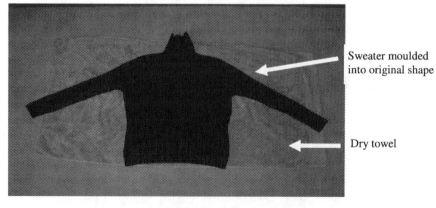

4. Presenting

Combinations

Purpose will guide you

The different forms of presenting information can be combined.
A Worksheet (with places for handwritten info) can combine
the steps of a Recipe with the Decision Table.

Example

Planning a business lunch

STEP	ACTION		
1	*Invite your guest to have lunch with you on a mutually convenient date.* *DATE:_____*		
2	**IF the guest is ...**	**THEN choose...**	*CHOICE:*
	• A new acquaintance	*an up-market restaurant*	
	• An old acquaintance *• Keen on sports*	*a sports bar*	
	• Fond of fast food *• Impressed by frugality*	*a food court*	
3	*If the restaurant takes reservations, make one.* *TIME:_____*		
4	*Telephone or email the guest and explain where and when you will meet.* *CONFIRMED ON:_____*		

Notice the decision table embedded in Step 2 of the recipe.

Page layout

Make each page appealing

Our readers—customers, staff, managers, the public—have overflowing Inboxes on both their actual and electronic desktops. Our challenge as writers is to get their attention, hold their attention, and when the need arises, to entice them to come back for more.

The product of your engaging, selecting, and presenting has a basic building block: the page. This can be paper or screen.

Think of each page as a stand-alone object. It can be a dense mass of words in well-constructed grammatically correct sentences, or it be chunked into separate pieces.

Cues and units

Every page of this Guidebook has cues (short headings in bold font) and units (text, table, or graphic). These are the building blocks of content. They present information in bite-sized chunks, and they make navigating the content easier and quicker. Cues also set up MS Word's automatic generation of a table of contents.

Our human brains function well when they are prepared for what they are about to encounter. When you are told in advance what to expect, you can imagine a "file folder" in your brain labelling itself and preparing to be filled with new information. Picture a child learning the meaning of a new word.

Cues and units reflect nature's force of Stimulus ⇨ Response. See cue ⇨ Read unit. The effect could also be: See cue ⇨ Skip unit. Either way, the reader gets to choose instantly whether that unit of information is relevant right now. Serving a similar function, a newspaper heading summarizes the content of an article and enables you to either read or skip the article.

One level up

Before we talk further about cues, notice that the cues on this page are: **Make each page appealing, Cues and units, One level up, Deriving cues.**

The first heading on this page, with its slightly larger font, is **Page Layout**. This is called a topic (or super-cue) because it's the headline for all subsequent cues. A complete topic might fit on a single page or spill over onto several. The first topic of this Guidebook is "Why people write." See how it appears in the table of contents.

4. Presenting

Deriving cues

Faced with much content (even one page can be a lot) that you need to write, break it into units of information and derive helpful cues. Cues should be concise and meaningful. Terms used should reflect unit content. We will show you what we mean.

Example 1

Before: This is a single, dense paragraph.

It has come to the attention of the Environment Committee that employees are generating a considerable amount of garbage when they eat "take-out" lunches at their desks. We have decided, in the interests of the environment, to install recycling bins on each floor near the elevators. The black wastebaskets at each desk will be removed. One bin will take plastics; a second will take cans and bottles; a third will take organic matter (banana peels, apple cores, etc.) for composting; the fourth will take non-recyclable waste. The containers will be ready for use on July 15th.

After: This is easier to read and remember as four units, each with its own cue.

Cue
Unit

Background

It has come to the attention of the Environment Committee that employees are generating a considerable amount of garbage when they eat "take-out" lunches at their desks.

Recycling bins

We have decided, in the interests of the environment, to install recycling bins on each floor near the elevators. The black wastebaskets at each desk will be removed.

Effective date

The following containers will be ready for use on July 15th.

Four types of waste

Bin #	Use for
1	*plastics*
2	*cans and bottles*
3	*organic matter (banana peels, apple cores, etc.) for composting*
4	*non-recyclable waste*

Choose cue words carefully so they reflect the content of the unit. (Words on the next page are only underlined for easy referral.)

4. Presenting

IF you are dealing with ...	THEN cue with words like ...
facts	• *Agenda for next meeting* • *Proposed development plan* • *People on the team* The underlined words are all nouns.
a process	• *The stages of XYZ certification* • *How the Insurance Plan works* • *The sale by tender process* The words "stages, how, and process" all denote process.
a procedure	• *How to change the filter* • *Operating the widget* • *Programming the ABC system* Notice the verbs.
an object	• *The XKE widget* • *Main control panel* • *Expense Account Form* These are all nouns.

Guidelines for cues

Be sure cues have these characteristics:

- **Concise:** Use as few words as you can get away with—so the cue is easy to scan as the eye reviews the page. Consider 5 the maximum number of words.

- **Consistent:** Use words that the reader will find in the unit.

- **Meaningful:** The cue should make sense without having to read the unit. Remember that the cues will be scanned for relevance.

- **Readable:** Make sparing use of all capitals. Besides readability, ALL CAPS GIVE THE READER THE FEELING THEY ARE BEING SHOUTED AT!

- **Visually separate:** In this text the cues are left-justified in a Style that differs from the rest of the text. This makes them easy to scan. If you do not wish to follow this convention, choose another way to visually separate cues from the unit (especially useful for email).

4. Presenting

Example

Here are three different ways to visually separate the cue, "Dogs make excellent pets" from the unit.

1. On separate line

Dogs make excellent pets

Choose a dog as a pet because they are always happy to see you and will love you no matter how crummy your day has been. You will get fit and healthy because you need to take them for many walks and your heart rate will decrease as you pet them. As a result, you will live a long and healthy life.

2. All capitals

DOGS MAKE EXCELLENT PETS: Choose a dog as a pet because they are always happy to see you and will love you no matter how crummy your day has been. You will get fit and healthy because you need to take them for many walks and your heart rate will decrease as you pet them. As a result, you will live a long and healthy life.

3. Bold & underlined

Dogs make excellent pets: Choose a dog as a pet because they are always happy to see you and will love you no matter how crummy your day has been. You will get fit and healthy because you need to take them for many walks and your heart rate will decrease as you pet them. As a result, you will live a long and healthy life.

One column with headings

The most straightforward cue/unit layout is one column, left justified, equal left and right margins. This Guidebook uses one column with left-indented headings.

Headings serve two purposes:

1. They break the content into bite-sized chunks that encourage and accommodate the reader. Dense text page after page tends to discourage all except the most motivated reader. If you depend on readers to be motivated, you will be writing for *in*action.

2. Second, they make it easier for the reader to find what they need by scanning the headings.

Headings and the table of contents

Headings, both cues and the one-level up topics, enable MS Word to generate a table of contents, such as the one at the front of this Guidebook. When you make revisions, you can instantly update the table of contents with a mouse-click.

Two columns

The two column layout has the headings in the left column and the text in the right. Here's how page 1 of this Guidebook would look if we were using this layout:

4. Presenting

Example 1

Why do <u>you</u> write?	If you write to keep in touch with others, to reach out and share your news and views, then *Just Do It!*
	But, if you write, or want to write, to influence what your readers think, how they feel, and what they do, then you need to:
	✓ engage them
	✓ equip them
	✓ guide them.
Why put it in writing?	Let's say you could speak to your audience. Would you bother to write? Should you bother to write?
	Yes and yes. Because …
	o there's only so much people will remember. If you are speaking to them—at a meeting for example—also give them a handout summarizing your message. Then you can concentrate on engaging them aloud, knowing that you have put in their hands the information they will need after the meeting.
	o you can organize the information exactly the way the user will need it when the time comes. So when the time comes to take action, the reader will be able to quickly find and easily follow your instructions. Call it just-in-time information.
	Also, there are many situations when you cannot speak to your audience because it would be too impractical. They may be spread across the company, across the city, or across the world.
	This book will help you write emails and letters, as well as instructions, meeting minutes, reports, and technical manuals.

4. Presenting

Example 2

Here is the "Deriving cues" example in 2 column layout:

Background	It has come to the attention of the Environment Committee that employees are generating a considerable amount of garbage when they eat "take-out" lunches at their desks.
Recycling bins	We have decided, in the interests of the environment, to install recycling bins on each floor near the elevators. The black wastebaskets at each desk will be removed.
Effective date	The following containers will be ready for use on July 15th.

Four types of waste	Bin #	Use for
	1	Plastics
	2	Cans and bottles
	3	Organic matter (banana peels, apple cores, etc.) for composting
	4	Non-recyclable waste

Pros & Cons of two columns

Pros	Cons
• Headings can be easily scanned • Plenty of white space helps reader	• Writer needs to use a Table, which requires handling of row and page breaks

4. Presenting

Visible gridlines

You have the option of making the gridlines visible. Here's how the previous Example 2 would look:

Example 3

Background	It has come to the attention of the Environment Committee that employees are generating a considerable amount of garbage when they eat "take-out" lunches at their desks.
Recycling bins	We have decided, in the interests of the environment, to install recycling bins on each floor near the elevators. The black wastebaskets at each desk will be removed.
Effective date	The following containers will be ready for use on July 15th.

Four types of waste	Bin #	Use for
	1	plastics
	2	cans and bottles
	3	organic matter (banana peels, apple cores, etc.) for composting
	4	non-recyclable waste

Pros & Cons of visible gridlines

Pros	Cons
• Helps the reader navigate the information more quickly	• Visual clutter may outweigh usefulness

You can opt for selected gridlines. In this case only horizontal are selected, which reduces visual clutter. The cues are not printed in **bold**.

4. Presenting

Example 4

Background	It has come to the attention of the Environment Committee that employees are generating a considerable amount of garbage when they eat "take-out" lunches at their desks.
Recycling bins	We have decided, in the interests of the environment, to install recycling bins on each floor near the elevators. The black wastebaskets at each desk will be removed.
Effective date	The following containers will be ready for use on July 15th.
Four types of waste	<table><tr><td><u>Bin #</u></td><td><u>Use for</u></td></tr><tr><td>1</td><td>plastics</td></tr><tr><td>2</td><td>cans and bottles</td></tr><tr><td>3</td><td>organic matter (banana peels, apple cores, etc.) for composting</td></tr><tr><td>4</td><td>non-recyclable waste</td></tr></table>

Finding information

Table of Contents

Let's say your content is well-selected and well-presented—on 2 pages or 20. You know that no reader is going to study and memorize your magnificent work. What you really want is that when the need arises, they will pick up your document and find the relevant bit.

How do you increases your chances they will pick up the document?

How do you increase their chances they will find what they need quickly?

One way is to create a table of contents. Having presented your information in bite-sized chunks of cues and units, you have Word generate a table of contents based on the styles you have used. Refer to your word processing application Help to make this happen.

4. Presenting

Subject Index

If you want to go the extra mile, you can also generate a subject index. Your subject matter and your audience may warrant this investment of your time. A subject index is helpful when there are many technical terms and inter-connected ideas, whether they be financial, legal, engineering, manufacturing, or other relatively complex content.

Since this Guidebook already presents information in bite-sized chunks listed in the Table of Contents, a subject index isn't quite warranted. However, one is provided as an example, with instructions for generating one in the Appendix.

Headers and Footers

Readers will often browse a document, even when there is a table of contents and a subject index. They will even flip pages in a massive document, such as the Yellow Pages. To assist browsers, the document should always be telling them, "You are here." This is the role of page headers and footers. They are the red dots on the mall map: "You are here." Don't you wish there were more of these in big buildings?

A further reason for headers and footers is that individual pages may get copied for others. The headers/footers will identify where the pages came from.

The absolute minimum for a document of 2 or more pages is page numbers, usually somewhere along the bottom edge.

Guideline for location

What to include on each page...	Where to put it...
Organization	header or footer
Publication/Document title	header
Chapter/Section title and/or number	header
Sub-section title and/or number	header
Edition/Version date and/or number (This helps when several people are working on the same document. It ensures that everyone is working on the latest version.)	footer
Author	footer
Page number	footer

4. Presenting

Perfecting comes later

Details promote stardom

At this point you've come a long way but you're not done yet. The last mile to accomplishing your purpose is where you attend to the details: sentence structure, voice, grammar, terminology, consistent style, precise words.

All this is covered in **Perfecting**. Perfection takes time, but the time to get there will get shorter with practice. You might even become a star among your peers, and a hero with your readers.

5. Perfecting

Active vs. passive

Comparisons

Passive voice: "The contract was signed by the manager."

Construction is <u>passive</u> when the object acted on (the contract) comes before the action (signed) and the actor (manager).

Active voice: "The manager signed the contract."

Construction is <u>active</u> with this order: actor, action, object acted on.

Passive: "An implementation plan was developed by the consultant."

Active: "The consultant developed an implementation plan."

We're so used to passive constructions, we sometimes don't notice our own passive sentences. To see the difference, ask yourself, "Who is doing what to whom?" If *the who* is the subject, you're probably in active voice.

Passive: "The first offer was accepted by the seller."

Active: "The seller accepted the first offer."

Why active is better

With rare exceptions, active voice is simpler, clearer, shorter. It states a "do" action instead of making a "done to" or "done by" statement.

From *Writing at Work: Professional Writing Skills for People on the Job,* Smith and Bernhardt:

"Knowing when to choose active or passive verb constructions goes right to the heart of developing a strong, vigorous writing style. Passive constructions sap energy from prose, leaving it bloated and flatulent. Active constructions allow your readers to see exactly who is doing what to whom. If you cultivate an active style, you are more likely to be understood.

Modifiers

Use sparingly

An adjective modifies a noun: "The *careless* homeowner acted as though…"

An adverb modifies a verb: "The homeowner acted *carelessly.*"

Using too many modifiers weakens your writing. Too many modifiers can be as annoying as a page on which every sentence has bolded words. The highlights lose their effect. In the case of modifiers, they lose effectiveness and clutter your writing.

Examples

Before	After
Although they may have "fallen in love" with a house they think is fabulous, first-time buyers should rely on their agent's experience and expertise to decide on an offer that fits their resources and earning power.	*First-time house buyers should rely on their agent's expertise when deciding the offer they can afford.*
Prospective buyers may be turned off by the personal touches the owner has installed, like displays of family photographs and collections of heirloom china or sports equipment.	*Buyers viewing a house are impressed by clean rooms free of clutter.*
This important, timely, and well-researched recommendation will allow us to more effectively and more quickly leverage the growing and currently under-utilized talent pool in the organization.	*This recommendation will power our talent to achieve new heights.*

There may be nuances missing in the 'after' statements, but you get the idea. Strong statements come with fewer words.

Brevity

Help your reader understand

When you know a lot about a subject and you want readers to care about it as you do, you've got a lot to say to them. Being brief is hard. In some respects it's unnatural.

Think of reading as opening brain files. At the start of a each paragraph, the reader opens a file in her brain and starts processing the words and ideas. The file closes when the reader has understood the paragraph.

The longer the paragraph and the more complex the sentences, the longer the reader has to keep the brain file open. The reader has to work harder to close the file successfully.

5. Perfecting

Watch sentence length

A paragraph should express one idea in a few sentences. Sentences should have roughly 10 to 15 words. Vary their length to keep the reader engaged. A sentence of 10 words is very easy to understand. Sentences containing more than 25 words will also contain many clauses and may require more than one reading for comprehension.

Example

From the Globe & Mail, March 29, 2008, page A20:

As the torch makes its slow journey around the world, passing through Beijing this weekend before crossing Asia, the Middle East, Europe and the Americas before returning to China for its controversial trip through Tibet in May, the three Canadian women are working their Blackberries and laptops late into the night, ensuring that something dramatic will happen at each stop.

This sentence consists of 60 words! If you really hunt, you will see that the Subject-Verb-Object of this sentence is, "Women working Blackberries." That's what your brain subconsciously looks for as you read the sentence. The more extra words there are, the harder your brain has to work to capture the accurate meaning.

Some writers who have not enjoyed the benefit of a university education seem to think that their writing will be more impressive and sophisticated if they construct lengthy sentences. In actual fact, the reverse is true. Shorter is better.

Consistent grammatical form

Make bullets match

A set of items in a list should have the same grammatical form, that is, all nouns, all participles, all action verbs, etc. Follow the same principle for chapter titles.

Examples

Inconsistent grammatical form	Consistent
We use this service because • *they deliver when promised* • *low prices* • *items are packaged securely.*	*We use this service because they:* • *deliver when promised* • *charge low prices* • *package items securely.* All begin with action verbs.

5. Perfecting

Inconsistent grammatical form	Consistent
My favourite pastimes: • *I like to walk my dog* • *Going sailing* • *A game of tennis*	*My favourite pastimes are:* • *walking my dog* • *going sailing* • *playing tennis.* All are participles.
Chapters in a car manual: • *All about the engine* • *How to check fluid levels* • *Keeping the body in top shape* • *Warning lights* • *Proper use of the HVAC system*	*Chapters in a car manual:* • *Engine components* • *Fluid level maintenance* • *Body care* • *Warning lights* • *HVAC system* All are nouns.
Replace the filter on the Filler when any of these situations occur: • *lumpy soap flakes* • *a box takes more than 20 seconds to be filled.* • *soap flakes piling up on the floor*	*Replace the filter on the Filler when any of these situations occur:* • *Soap flakes are lumpy.* • *It takes more than 20 seconds to fill a box.* • *A pile of soap flakes forms on the floor.* All are complete sentences.

Precision with words

Nouns rule

Sometimes a single noun will replace a phrase, clause, or multiple modifiers.

This Guidebook is covering the writing of emails and business documents. These suggestions of brevity and precision with words are *not* appropriate for creative writers who seek to entertain their readers.

Examples

Was written like this	How about ...
Highly achievement-oriented, without displaying weakness or uncertainty	*strength*

5. Perfecting

Was written like this	How about ...
Dedication to overcoming all obstacles and difficulties encountered	*motivation*
Certain that he is on the right path, in fact the only path, to success	*conviction*
With obnoxious conceit and total self-centeredness	*narcissism*
Absolutely positive and beyond any doubt	*certainty*

Casting the sentence

Easily understood sentences have the Subject-Verb-Object (SVO) form.

Example 1

The dog chased the cat.

The manager praised the employee.

The writer finished the article.

Sentences get complicated when the SVO form is cluttered with modifiers.

Example 2

The figures in the second quarter report corroborate our view that sales have increased in global markets.

The underlined words are the subject-verb-object. The rest are all modifiers.

One way to add clarity is to extract the SVO and then state the rest:

The figures corroborate our view: second quarter sales have increased in global markets.

Example 3

Before

As the updates are now complete, the financial planning system will be rolled out as soon as the representatives of each region contact Head Office.

After

Attention regional representatives: the updated financial planning system is ready for rollout. Please contact Head Office promptly.

5. Perfecting

Consistent terminology

Different terms for the same thing can confuse readers. If you start out writing about "invoices," later refer to "bills," then give instructions for "statements," the reader may not know whether these are the same or different things. Figuring it out is a waste of time.

Consistency also helps when you want to clearly differentiate among actions. For example, you can consistently say "type" for only entering data, "enter" for filling in a field <u>and</u> pressing an enter button, "press" for pressing a keyboard key, and "click" to activate an on-screen button or box. By using these terms consistently, you can be concise with your instructions and the reader can be certain of your intent. STOP HERE

Dealing with he/she/they

Be inclusive

When referring to members of both genders (male and female), we need to refer to both "he and "she" in order to be inclusive. There are three ways to deal with this quandary, starting with the most desirable:

1. Always write in the plural form.
   Example: Investors usually want to maximize contributions to their Registered Retirement Savings Plans.

2. Alternate units, pages, or chapters using all "he" or all "she."

3. Use both genders.
   Example: Each investor must receive his/her T5s before the end of the month.

Common grammatical errors

Incorrect	Correct
The policy covers my wife and I.	*The policy covers my wife and <u>me</u>.*
	Explanation: "me" is the *object* of the verb covers. "I" is the *subject* form.
	To check this, mentally remove "my wife" from the sentence, and ask yourself if "The policy covers I" sounds correct. It does not.

Incorrect	Correct
Its important that we accept all it's rules and procedures.	*It's important that we accept all <u>its</u> rules and procedures.*
	Explanation: "It's stands for "It is" and "its" is the possessive pronoun (like his, her).
The document posted on the website is particularly useful because of its accuracy.	*The document, particularly useful because of its accuracy, is posted on the website.*
	In the original sentence, "*its accuracy*" would refer to the nearest referent, the website. Place the pronoun closest to its intended referent.

Punctuation basics

Commas

Commas are used to indicate a natural pause in speech. If you were reading the sentence aloud, a comma tells you where to insert a slight pause.

Example 1

> ✘ *The Prime Minister said "Who leaked this memo to the press?"*

> ✔ *The Prime Minister said, "Who leaked this memo to the press?"*

> ✘ *The horse bolted from the starting gate collided with another and went on to win the race.*

> ✔ *The horse bolted from the starting gate, collided with another, and went on to win the race.*

Commas separate a series of 3 or more items. Focus on the comma separating "white" from "and."

Example 2

> *Many countries use the colours red, white, and blue in their flags.*

> *The course covers real estate law, evaluating a property, handling a listing, and helping clients make a purchase.*

5. Perfecting

Commas prevent misinterpretation.

Example 3

- ☒ *The panda bear eats, shoots, and leaves.* This describes a ridiculous scene.
- ☑ *The panda bear eats shoots and leaves.* This describes a panda's diet of eucalyptus.

Commas join two complete sentences.

Don't take a chance when travelling, buy insurance before you leave.

It is tempting to avoid realtor's fees, handling the sale of your own home can be risky.

Bullets

In a list following a stem sentence with a colon (:), bullets start each item. Bullets act like commas in a list written this way. Remove the commas and the "and." End the sentence with a period.

Incorrect	Correct
My favourite sports are:	*My favourite sports are:*
• *canoeing,*	• *canoeing*
• *golf,*	• *golf*
• *tennis, and,*	• *tennis*
• *skiing*	• *skiing.*

Avoid visual clutter.

Quotations

Place commas and periods inside the final quotation mark.

Example 1

He said, "That idea is fabulous."

The candidate smiled and responded, "I have not chosen a running mate."

Place exclamation marks either inside or outside the final quotation mark, as appropriate to the intended meaning.

Example 2

The Queen cried out, "Off with his head!"

I was surprised to hear the Queen mutter to herself, "Let them eat cake"!

Text formatting

Bold, italics, underline

NOTE: Elsewhere in this Guidebook, examples are written in italics. Within this unit, that convention has been dismissed in order to clearly demonstrate the impact of bold, italics and underline.

Bold, or boldface, is great for **headings** and **emphasis**. Use it to highlight the key word or phrase that emphasizes the message or distinguishes the intent.

Examples

Okay	Better
When removing a jammed piece of toast, always unplug the toaster first.	When removing a jammed piece of toast, always **unplug** the toaster first.
We need to mail out T4s to all employees before February 28.	We need to mail out T4s to all employees **before February 28**.

Italics are perfect for quotes and for more subtle emphasis.

Examples

Okay	Better
Be sure to meet me at the north entrance of the subway station.	Be sure to meet me at the *north* entrance of the subway station.
Think of your initial offer as your only chance to make an impression, as the seller will probably receive several offers to purchase at the same time.	Think of your initial offer as your *only chance* to make an impression, as the seller will probably receive several offers to purchase at the same time.
He is not too interested in following up with this applicant as she is overqualified.	He is not too interested in following up with this applicant as she is *overqualified.*

5. Perfecting

Underlining should be used on a word or a few only as it adds visual clutter.

Examples

Okay	Better
Be sure to take your passport with you to the airport.	Be sure to take your passport with you to the airport.
The people who suffer the most from family conflict are the children.	The people who suffer the most from family conflict are the children.

When writing instructions, decide in advance which features you will use for which purpose, and then *apply the rules consistently*. For example, you may decide to use **bold** for all safety issues (unplugging, pouring carefully, checking labels, etc.) and *italics* when the reader needs to make a choice (adding nuts or cranberries, etc.)

Sometimes it's okay to combine 2 of the 3 features:

Bold italics is a good combination because *italics* are visually lighter than regular text. At a glance, a reader might not notice the italicized word(s).

Bold underlined is acceptable, but why bother. In text, the underline is overkill. In headings, just make the bold font bigger to increase prominence.

Underlined italics is also acceptable, but the underline seems redundant.

All three like this: ***Bold underlined italics*** ? Never.

Capitalization and ALL CAPS

Capitalization follows three main conventions:

- The beginning of sentences
- Proper nouns such as names
- Titles in text

Titles have 2 main styles:

- Sentence case wherein only the first word and proper nouns are capitalized
- Title Case Wherein All Words Are Capitalized.

(There is also ALL CAPS described on the next page.)

The downside of Title Case is that it will disguise proper nouns (e.g. city, brand, product names) in the title. When the proper noun is a key factor, it can go unnoticed.

5. Perfecting

Example

Why Band Aids Are Better Than Other Bandages

As we shall now see, in Sentence case, the point of the title is more evident:

Why Band Aids are better than other bandages

In Title Case, these words are <u>not</u> capitalized:

- articles *(a, the)*
- conjunctions of fewer than four letters *(and, but)*
- prepositions of fewer than four letters.*(in, on)*

… *unless* it is the first or last word in the title or follows a colon or dash.

ALL CAPS TEXT IS MORE DIFFICULT TO READ. THE THEORY IS THAT THE FEATURES OF LOWER CASE LETTERS, SUCH AS POINTS AND STEMS, OFFER GREATER VISUAL VARIATION THAN THE CONSTANT HEIGHT AND WEIGHT OF UPPER CASE LETTERS.

ALL CAPS text is more difficult to read. The theory is that the features of lower case letters, such as points and stems, offer greater visual variation than the constant height and weight of upper case letters.

That said, a SHORT TITLE IN ALL CAPS is quite alright.

Font selection

Popular fonts

The two most popular fonts in the English-speaking world are Times New Roman and Arial (True Type fonts). In Postscript printer language, these are called Times Roman and Helvetica. Text in this Guidebook is Times New Roman and titles are Arial.

There are hundreds of fonts. Two or three fonts are sufficient for most documents. Even the glitziest marketing piece will seldom exceed four.

The same font should be used for a hierarchy.

Example

NOTE: Elsewhere in this Guidebook, examples are written in italics. Within this unit, that convention has been dismissed in order to clearly demonstrate the impact of font selection.

This Guidebook has 3 sizes of headings (section, topic, cue) which are all Arial. The text is in Times New Roman.

5. Perfecting

Font types

There are three broad types of fonts: serif, sans serif, and script.

Serif fonts have little "ticks" at the bottom and tops of letters. An example is Times New Roman.

Sans serif fonts do <u>not</u> have these little "ticks." An example is Arial.

Reading research indicates that serif fonts are easier to read. The little ticks seem to act as guiderails for the eyes.

A serif font appears to be the dominant choice of newspaper, magazine, and book publishers. A san-serif font appears to be the dominant choice for websites. Corporate writers seem to like Arial.

Some sans-serif fonts have the problem of the capital "I" (comes after H) being identical to the lowercase l (comes after k).

What do readers prefer? A limited poll of e-book on-screen readers has 70% voting for the serif font. A larger on-line survey of Time New Roman versus Arial by a web marketing firm (1,643 respondents) shows a 2-1 vote in favour of Arial.

What should you choose for body text? Unless you are going to do the research, you could just go with the flow of publishers who might know something you don't. This means serif for printed page, sans serif for digital screen. Interestingly, the mighty Microsoft has the default for Word (printed page) as Times New Roman, and the default for Outlook (digital screen) as Arial.

Script fonts are fine for personal writing, such as invitations, and for marketing.

Font sizes

For most audiences, a text font between 10 and 12 point works well. A seniors audience will appreciate larger type. A student audience won't mind 9 point; they're used to even smaller fonts on websites.

Two to four sizes of heading fonts should suffice. This Guidebook uses four sizes: one for chapter titles and a 3-size hierarchy for section headings.

Readers will remember perhaps 4 sizes in a headings hierarchy, that is, they will know from the font size what level they are at. More than four sizes won't help the reader much.

5. Perfecting

Proofreading

Another pair of eyes

Ask others to proofread your document. Even if they don't understand the subject matter, you'll be surprised how often they find errors and inconsistencies even though you have already proofread it yourself. Professional proofreaders will search the document for only one or two items at a time, and repeat until all items have been addressed.

Checklist

When proofreading, these items need to be checked:

- Spelling mistakes
- Missing words
- Unnecessary spaces
- Grammar mistakes
- Sentence length
- Inconsistencies in features (use of **bold**, *italics*, <u>underlining</u>)
- Inconsistencies in headers, footers, page numbering

6. Sharpening your skills

This section contains exercises to help you sharpen your skills. They cover one or more aspects of *Writing for Action*™. You can write your answers in the spaces provided. Sample answers are provided in the Feedback .

Yours may differ a little or a lot from the sample. Don't be too hard on yourself. The important lesson is to recognize the good qualities in your writing, the good qualities in the book answer, and where you would do better next time. If you are not sure where something came from in the book answer, you might want to scan the relevant text to review specific points.

Precision exercises

Exercise 1: Rewrite these rules for teaching someone a task

Before	After
The learner should be positioned so that he or she can see what you are doing from the same angle as you.	
A brief explanation by you of what you are doing and why is appropriate.	
Leaving out mental steps should be avoided.	
The use of ordinary language and the explanation of technical terms are helpful.	
Key points should be emphasized.	
It is important that the learner try doing the task.	
Encouragement is important.	
As you go along, you should reduce the amount of coaching and give the learner a chance to practice.	

6. Sharpening your skills

Exercise 2: Replace each phrase with a word or two

Before	After
It is our opinion that	
It is necessary that we	
In view of the aforementioned	
We are in receipt of	
It is our intention to	
The results of analyzing the data shows that	
It is apparent to the committee and to me	
It is incumbent on us	
The study produced its data early	
This is to advise all recipients of this letter that they should	
We gave consideration to	
All of us managers are prepared	
We request that you do not	
It goes without saying that	
The company is responsible for gathering data, analysis, decisions, and implementing	

6. Sharpening your skills

Grammar exercises

Exercise 3: Rewrite this paragraph to make it easier for first time homebuyers to understand.

Before

Most first time homebuyers feel overwhelmed at the prospect of making a selection from the bewildering array of houses and condos, especially because they do not have as much money as the media tells them they need. Panic must be avoided at all costs because people will find themselves either moving too quickly (buying the first thing they see) or missing out over and over again because they dawdle or try to get an unrealistic bargain. I implore you to take your time. Its too easy to fall in love without being prepared.

After

Exercise 4: Rewrite this paragraph to make it easier for bank employees to understand.

Before

It has been decided that postponement of the publication of the new policy to the start of the year will be a necessary delay because the modification of the standards will cause difficulties and added expense, leading to increased frustration on the part of the customers in the foreseeable future.

After

6. Sharpening your skills

Exercise 5: Rewrite this announcement to make it easier for members of a sailing club to understand.

Before

There is a need to plan the summer events for our sailing club. The president and me are interested in meeting everyones needs as much as possible, so its important that you think about the next summer although its a long way off. Ask yourself "What would I sign up for" and "I'd like to be involved in organizing that event". Your input is greatly encouraged.

We need to figure out:

- The entry fee for each regatta,
- Just how to decide who can enter each regatta,
- How many prizes to get,
- To handle the officiating and running of each regatta.

The suggestions you submit to Reception written on paper will be sent to him and I via email. Go to the club website next month to see the committee's recommendation and use it to volunteer your services.

After:

Feedback

Exercise 1

Before	After
The learner should be positioned so that he or she can see what you are doing from the same angle as you.	*Position the learner to see the task from the same angle.*
A brief explanation by you of what you are doing and why is appropriate.	*Explain briefly what you are doing and why.*
Leaving out mental steps should be avoided.	*Don't leave out mental steps.*
The use of ordinary language and the explanation of technical terms are helpful.	*Use ordinary language. Explain technical terms.*
Key points should be emphasized.	*Emphasize key points.*
It is important that the learner try doing the task.	*Let the learner try doing the task.*
Encouragement is important.	*Encourage.*
As you go along, you should reduce the amount of coaching and give the learner a chance to practice.	*Reduce coaching. Allow practice.*

Exercise 2

Before	After
It is our opinion that …	*We believe …*
It is necessary that we …	*We must …*
In view of the aforementioned …	*Therefore …*
We are in receipt of …	*We received …*
It is our intention to …	*We intend to …*

6. Sharpening your skills

Before	After
The results of analyzing the data shows that ...	*The analysis shows that ...*
It is apparent to the committee and to me that ...	*The committee and I see that ...*
It is incumbent on us ...	*We should ...*
The data coming out of the study in this early period indicates ...	*The early data shows ...*
This is to advise all recipients of this letter that they should ...	*Please ...*
We gave consideration to ...	*We considered ...*
We request that you do not ...	*Please do not ...*
It goes without saying that ...	*Obviously ...*
The company is responsible for gathering data, analysis, decisions, and implementing	*The company is responsible for gathering and analyzing data, making decisions and implementing new policies.*

Exercise 3: Rewrite this paragraph to make it easier for first time homebuyers to understand.

Before

Most first time homebuyers feel overwhelmed at the prospect of making a selection from the bewildering array of houses and condos, especially because they do not have as much money as the media tells them they need. Panic must be avoided at all costs because people will find themselves either moving too quickly (buying the first thing they see) or missing out over and over again because they dawdle or try to get an unrealistic bargain. I implore you to take your time. Its too easy to fall in love without being prepared.

After

As a first time homebuyer on a budget, you are probably a little overwhelmed by all the choices available to you. Before you visit any homes, work closely with your agent to define your needs and preferences. This decreases the possibility of your "falling in love" with a house you cannot afford.

6. Sharpening your skills

Exercise 4: Rewrite this paragraph to make it easier for bank employees to understand.

<u>Before</u>

It has been decided that postponement of the publication of the new policy to the start of the year will be a necessary delay because the modification of the standards will cause difficulties and added expense, leading to increased frustration on the part of the customers in the foreseeable future.

<u>After</u>

(WHAT) The new policy will be published at the start of the year. (WHY) This will give us time to adjust internally to the new standards and avoid involving the customers in the transition.

Exercise 5: Rewrite this announcement to make it easier for members of a sailing club to understand.

<u>Before</u>

There is a need to plan the summer events for our sailing club. The president and me are interested in meeting everyones needs as much as possible, so its important that you think about the next summer although its a long way off. Ask yourself "What would I sign up for" and "I'd like to be involved in organizing that event". Your input is greatly encouraged.

We need to figure out:

- The entry fee for each regatta,
- Just how to decide who can enter each regatta,
- How many prizes to get,
- To handle the officiating and running of each regatta.

The suggestions you submit to Reception written on paper will be sent to him and I via email. Go to the club website next month to see the committee's recommendation and use it to volunteer your services.

<u>After</u>

We need to plan the summer events for our sailing club. The president and I are interested in meeting everyone's needs as much as possible, so it's important that you think about next summer, although it's a long way off. Ask yourself, "What would I sign up for?" and "I'd like to be involved in organizing that event." Your input is greatly encouraged and much appreciated.

We need to figure out:

- *The entry fee for each regatta*
- *Who can enter each regatta*
- *Number of prizes*

6. Sharpening your skills

- *Who will officiate and run each regatta.*

The suggestions you submit to Reception written on paper will be sent to the president and me via email. Next month, read the committee's recommendation on the club website and use it to volunteer your services.

Appendix

Recipe checklist

- ☐ Name the task.

- ☐ Speak to the reader using action verbs (e.g. Place, Press).

- ☐ Use "NOTE:" to separate additional information from the action.

- ☐ Use "Result:" to separate the result from the action.

- ☐ If the step contains several items, list with bullet points.

- ☐ Use a consistent format to represent item in the same class (e.g. fields on a screen, parts of equipment)

- ☐ Place "if" condition at the beginning of a step.

- ☐ Highlight only critical words with bold, italics, underline, or all capitals. Be consistent.

- ☐ Make each step small enough so the reader is able to do it without having to re-read it.

- ☐ Stay within the range of 5 to 9 steps. If you have more steps, then group them into major steps or phases.

Decision table checklist

- ☐ Name the task.
- ☐ Speak to the reader.
- ☐ Allocate a column for each condition and action.
- ☐ Order the variables in columns left to right:
  - IFs (conditions) before the THENs (actions)
  - The stimuli before the responses.
  - Use arrows across empty boxes.

  Example: In the decision table for selling cigarettes, the customer's age is estimated before I.D. is requested.

- ☐ Order the situations and outcomes by frequency of occurrence in rows top to bottom

  Example: Since most customers will appear to be at least 21 years old, that row is at the top of the table.

- ☐ Eliminate repetition by pulling common elements into the column headings. If the same leading words appear in several cells, move them up to the header.

- ☐ Check that each row is a correct and complete decision.

Appendix

Report writing cue menu

For this type of reports	These cues may work	
Minutes of a meeting	• Date of meeting • Purpose of meeting • Attendees • Agenda or topics covered	• Decisions made • Action needed • Next meeting
Proposal	• Background • Objectives • Approach • Benefits	• Schedule • Cost estimate • Project staff • Terms and conditions
Feasibility report	• Background • Problem • Methods of investigation • Assumptions • Findings	• Solutions • Benefits • Cost • Recommendations • Rationale
Status report	• Status (schedule, cost) • Personnel involved • Tasks completed • Future actions	• Problems • Solutions • Decision needed

<u>Appendix</u>

Slide Presentation Tips

Keep it simple

- ✓ Slides make the points, YOU tell the story
- ✓ 7 points (not sentences) max, with 7-10 words each
- ✓ Simple language
- ✓ Simple cumulative builds (point 4 of 7 slide shows points 1-4 with 4 highlighted)
- ✓ 2 font types sufficient, sans serif
- ✓ 3 font sizes sufficient, minimum 20 pt
- ✓ Sparing use of ALL CAPS, *italics*, <u>underlines</u>
- ✓ Common or symbolic bullets, not artsy ones
- ✓ Simple graphics that make 1-3 key points
- ✓ Maximum of 3 colours for text or 5 for graphics. Use colour for distinction, not decoration
- ✓ Simple transition effect, or none

What audiences find annoying[1]

Speaker reads slides	62%
Text too small	47%
Hard to read colour selections	43%
Full sentences instead of bullet points	39%
Fancy transition effects	25%
Overly complex graphics	22%

---

[1] Source: What Annoys Audiences About PowerPoint Presentations? Dave Paradi, MBA, The PowerPoint Lifeguard

Appendix

Connecting with your audience

When a slide appears, audience will be busy scanning.

Either pause before speaking, or speak for 10 seconds before making a key point

Average pace: 0.5 – 2 min per slide, averaging 1 min/slide max

Pause slides and have a Q&A or discussion break every 10-15 min

Face the audience and look at the laptop screen, not the projector screen behind you.

Appendix

PowerPoint Basics

This illustration is based on PowerPoint 2003

Start a new presentation

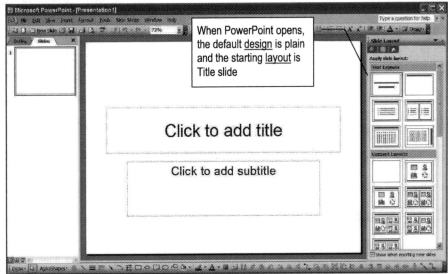

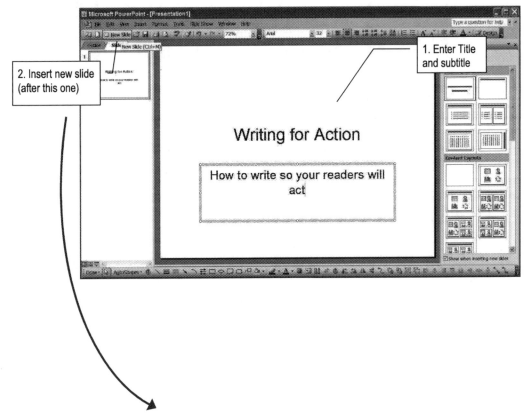

Appendix

Create slides

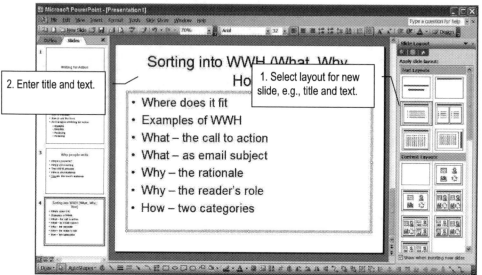

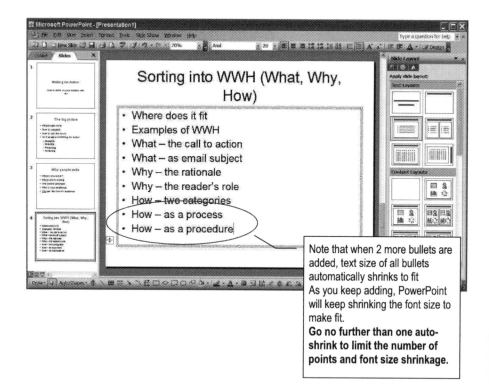

Appendix

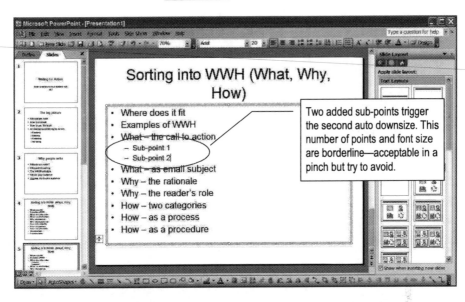

Apply a design template

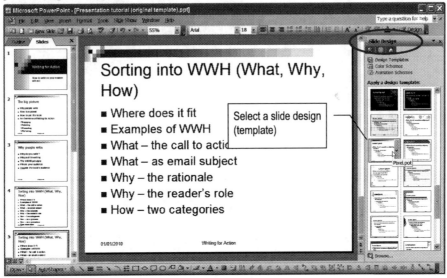

Appendix

Customize the design

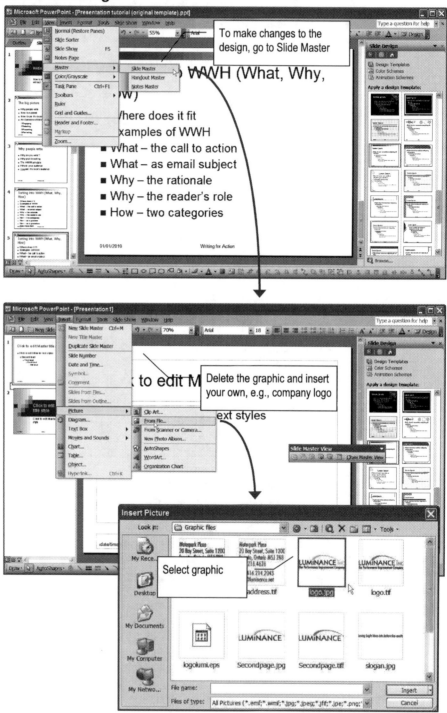

Appendix

Your logo will appear on every slide

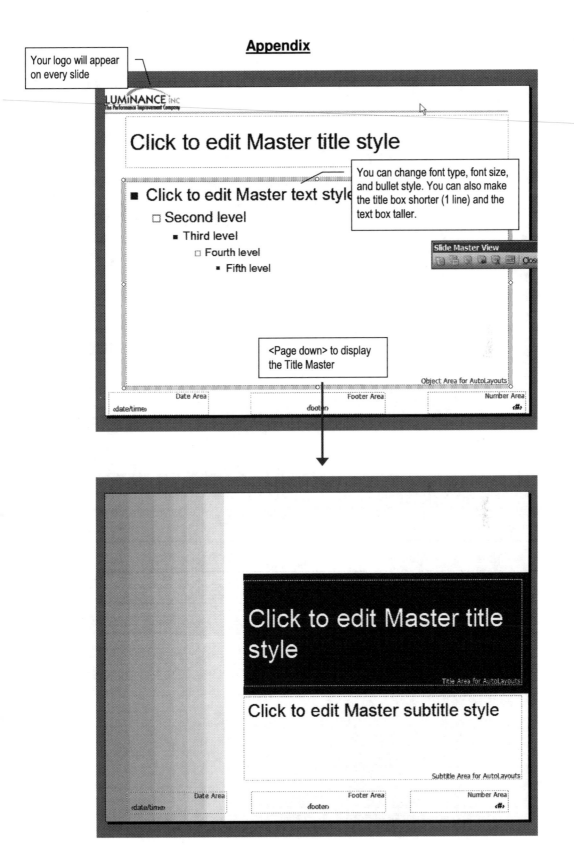

Click to edit Master title style

You can change font type, font size, and bullet style. You can also make the title box shorter (1 line) and the text box taller.

- Click to edit Master text style
  - Second level
    - Third level
      - Fourth level
        - Fifth level

<Page down> to display the Title Master

Object Area for AutoLayouts

Slide Master View

Date Area | Footer Area | Number Area
‹date/time› | ‹footer› | ‹#›

Click to edit Master title style

Title Area for AutoLayouts

Click to edit Master subtitle style

Subtitle Area for AutoLayouts

Date Area | Footer Area | Number Area
‹date/time› | ‹footer› | ‹#›

Appendix

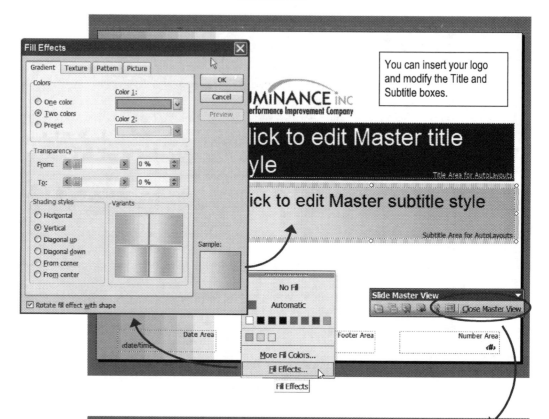

You can insert your logo and modify the Title and Subtitle boxes.

Appendix

Insert footers

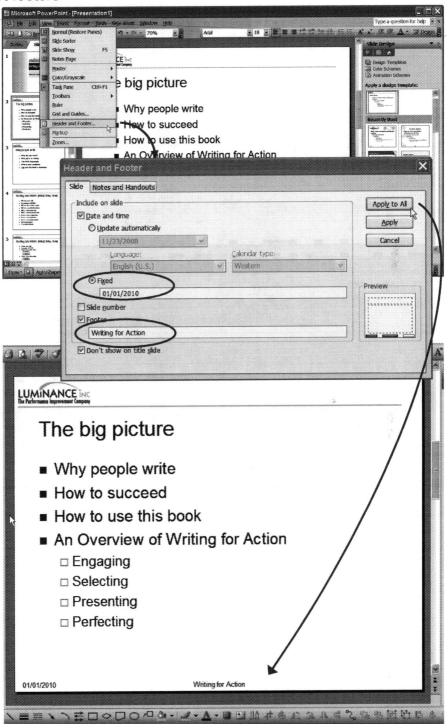

Appendix

Preparing presentation notes

Slide notes help you to:

- ✓ keep the slide simple
- ✓ tell the story you want to
- ✓ provide a more detailed handout if you wish

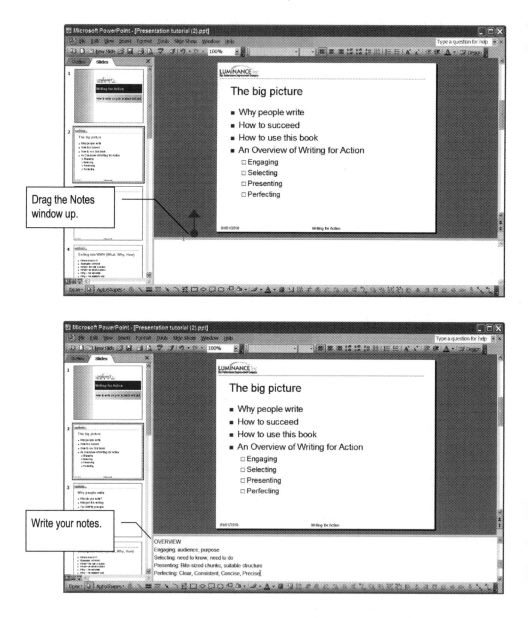

Appendix

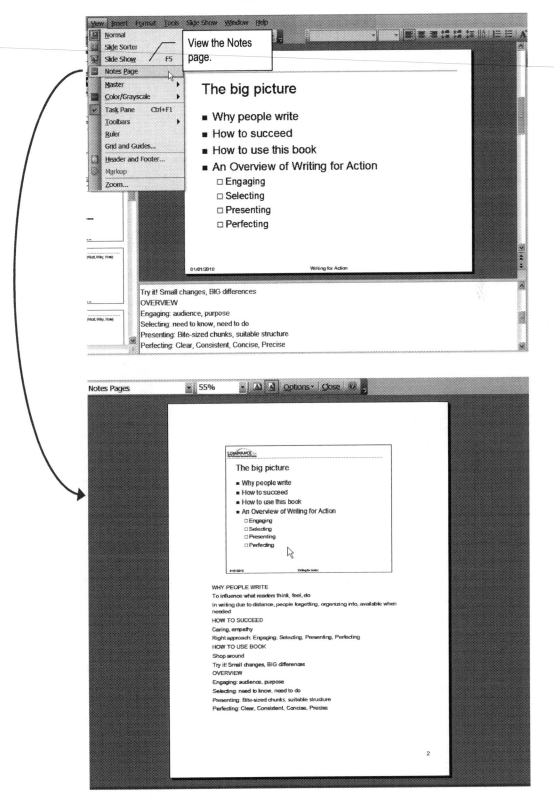

Appendix

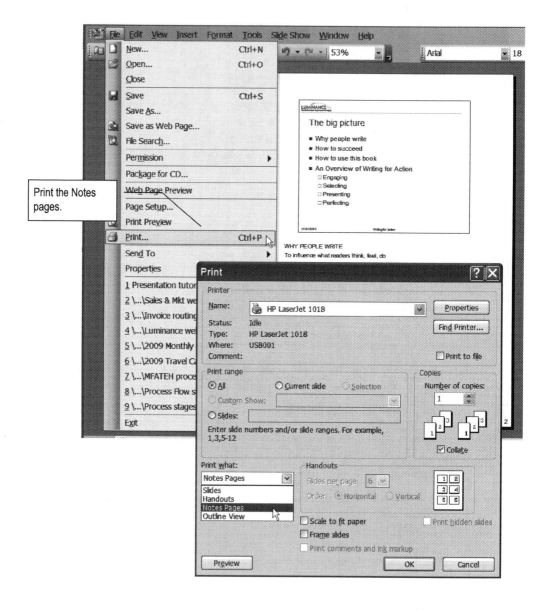

Print the Notes pages.

Appendix

Creating a subject index

The method shown here is for Word 2003. The process will be similar for other versions of Word.

Create a concordance file

Here's what the one for this Guidebook looks like:

Term	Index entry
act	action
action	action
actions	action
active	active
active vs. passive	active vs. passive
adjective	adjective
adjectives	adjective
adverb	adverb
adverbs	adverb
all caps	capital letters
attention	attention
audience	audience
bite-size	bite-size
bite-sized	bite-size
brevity	brevity
bullet	bullets
bulleted	bullets
bullets	bullets

The full table continues from C to Z.

Steps

1. Start a two-column table. You can name the columns whatever you want.

2. In the first column, enter the word, term, or phrase you want to index.
   Here's how: scan through your document text. When you see something you want to index, enter it in the first column. Ignore alphabetical order.

3. Sort the table alphabetically. This will reveal where you entered the identical item more than once. By ignoring possible repetition, you will complete Step 2 faster.

4. Enter variants of terms if you want Word to include them, e.g., singular/plural, present/past tense, etc.

5. In the second column, enter what you want to appear in the index for that word/term/phrase in the first column. For example, wherever Word finds the first three words (act, action, actions), it will index all those instances under <u>one</u> term: **action**. Similarly, all instances of "bullet, bulleted, bullets" will be indexed as <u>one</u> entry, "bullet". Meaningful consolidation makes the subject index more compact and easier to use.

6. Save your concordance file.

Mark the entries in your document

1. Open your document.

2. On the menubar, Go to Insert / Reference / Index and Tables

3. In the Index tab, click Automark ..., select your concordance file, Open.
   Word will find and "mark" all the terms you have specified in the first column of the concordance file.

Generate the index

1. If indexing codes {XE "action"} are visible in your document, hide them to preserve your page endings and pages. To hide, go to Tools / Options / View tab Formatting marks section and de-select "Hidden text", OK.

2. Position the cursor in your document where you want the subject index to appear.

3. On the menubar, Go to Insert / Reference / Index and Tables

4. In the Index tab, specify the number of columns (this Guidebook uses 3) and OK to generate the subject index.

You can try other Formats: in the Index and Tables / Index tab.

- To re-generate the index, repeat steps 3-4 with the new format selected.

- If your cursor was somewhere in the subject index, you will be asked whether to replace it or cancel the action.

- If your cursor is elsewhere in the document, you will be asked whether to replace the existing index, Yes or No, or cancel. No will generate another index where the cursor was.

You can also format the index manually as you would any document content, e.g., Format / Columns to change the number of columns, the space between columns, etc.

Update the index

At anytime, after modifying/editing your document, right-click (right mouse button) in the index and select Update Field. If you had done some manual formatting, you will need to re-do it.

If you modify the concordance file, re-do the **Mark the entries** steps first.

Writing Planner

My audience (Who) What's noteworthy, special, or different about them?	
My stated purpose (What) What do I want them to do (or think or feel)?	
Their WIIFM (Why) Why should they care?	
What do they already know about this?	
What do I need to provide? (How)	
Where, from whom can I get information?	
Who should review?	

Appendix

Writing Checklist

- ☐ Clear on who my audience is
- ☐ Purpose of my writing to them upfront and clear
- ☐ WIIFM included
- ☐ What audience already knows taken into account
- ☐ All content filtered for relevance, nothing there can be left out to make more concise
- ☐ Paragraphs converted to bullets where suitable
- ☐ Statements put in table format where suitable
- ☐ Procedure or instructions written in active voice (do this, do that …)
- ☐ Illustrations used where helpful
- ☐ Flowcharts used for technical audiences and like others
- ☐ Information presented in bite-sized chunks with cues (headings) and units (text blocks)
- ☐ Table of contents provided with lengthy documents
- ☐ Headers and footers, page numbers, version/date added where helpful
- ☐ Active voice preferred over passive voice
- ☐ Short to moderate sentences used; long sentences divided into two sentences
- ☐ Modifiers used modestly to keep writing uncluttered
- ☐ Items in a list take the same grammatical form (all nouns, all actions, all participles (--ing), all full sentences, etc.)
- ☐ Terminology is consistent—the same term is used for the same thing
- ☐ Punctuation is consistent, e.g., comma or not before last item in a series, punctuation or not in bulleted list
- ☐ Punctuation is correct, e.g., periods and question marks inside quotation marks
- ☐ Capitalization is consistent, e.g., first word or all words in headings capitalized, official names capitalized, regular terms not capitalized, etc.
- ☐ Font size is appropriate to audience, e.g., minimum 10 pt, larger for older audience
- ☐ Font types limited to one or two, e.g., Times Roman for text, Arial for headings
- ☐ Document proofread by 2nd party
- ☐ Document to be distributed electronically converted to pdf to protect from changes or to ensure pages stay intact as intended

Subject Index

action, 1, 2, 3, 4, 6, 10, 11, 13, 14, 16, 17, 18, 19, 26, 32, 44, 46, 49, 51, 55, 65, 66, 79, 80, 83

active, 44, 79, 83

active vs. passive, 79

adjective, 44, 79

adverb, 44, 79

attention, 2, 3, 5, 6, 16, 19, 20, 34, 35, 39, 40, 41, 79

audience, 1, 2, 3, 4, 5, 9, 10, 12, 13, 16, 19, 20, 21, 38, 42, 55, 68, 79, 82, 83

bite-size, 3, 6, 21, 27, 34, 37, 41, 42, 79, 83

brevity, 47, 79

bullets, 19, 21, 22, 23, 26, 46, 51, 65, 67, 79, 80, 83

capital letters, 79

capitalizing, 27, 36, 37, 65

categories, 17, 29

checklist, 23, 65

clarity, 3, 4, 21, 28, 48, 83

concise, 3, 4, 35, 49, 83

connecting, 13, 16, 24

consistency, 3, 4, 26, 27, 43, 65, 83

content, 3, 5, 6, 13, 14, 16, 19, 20, 23, 24, 34, 35, 37, 41, 42, 81, 83

cues, 6, 34, 35, 36, 37, 39, 40, 41, 54, 66, 83

decision table, 31, 33, 65

direction, 6

empathy, 3

engaging, 1, 3, 5, 6, 10, 34, 38

feedback, 7, 11

filtering, 18, 19, 23, 36, 47, 83

flowchart, 21, 32

font, 23, 34, 53, 54, 55, 67

footer, 42, 56, 75, 83

formatting, 26, 52, 65, 80, 81, 83

gathering, 14, 17, 19, 58, 62

grammar, 43, 49

grouping, 22, 65

header, 42, 56, 65

headings, 1, 20, 34, 37, 52, 53, 54, 55, 65, 83

hierarchy, 6, 24, 54, 55

illustrations, 69

inclusive, 19, 49

Index entry, 79

indexing, 42, 79, 80, 81

influence, 1, 2, 9, 38

know your audience, 12

language, 3, 5, 6, 10, 54, 57, 61, 67

layout, 34, 37, 39

lettering, 23

modifiers, 44, 47, 48

motivation, 16, 17, 48

nouns, 36, 44, 46, 47, 53, 83

numbering, 24, 27, 42, 56

page numbering, 24, 42, 56, 83

paragraphs, 19, 21, 22, 25, 35, 45, 46, 59, 62, 63

passive, 44, 83

perfecting, 3, 6, 52

precise, 3, 4, 6, 43

presentations, 6, 69, 76

presenting, 3, 6, 13, 18, 25, 27, 29, 33, 34, 80

procedures, 11, 18, 23, 25, 32, 36, 50

processes, 10, 17, 29, 30, 32, 36, 79

proofreading, 56, 83

punctuation, 83

purpose, 2, 3, 4, 5, 10, 12, 19, 43, 53, 82

quotations, 51, 83

rationale, 14, 16

reading ability, 9

recipes, 25, 33

relevance, 14, 16, 18, 19, 20, 34, 36, 41, 57, 83

reports, 1, 4, 48, 66

research, 9, 27, 55

retention, 27

risks, 12, 16

selecting, 3, 5, 14, 15, 26, 34, 54, 59, 62, 80, 81

sentence length, 46

sentences, 12, 21, 22, 23, 25, 31, 34, 43, 44, 45, 46, 47, 48, 49, 50, 51, 53, 67, 83

sequence, 6, 24

structure, 4, 13, 21, 25, 43

subject, 6, 9, 12, 13, 14, 16, 42, 44, 45, 48, 49, 56, 79, 80

table of content, 4, 34, 37, 41, 42

tables, 4, 18, 21, 25, 29, 31, 33, 34, 37, 41, 42, 65, 79, 80, 83

terminology, 19, 43, 49

testing, 20

tone, 5

units, 6, 34, 35, 36, 37, 41, 49, 52, 54, 83

visual, 6, 23, 32, 40, 51, 53, 54

WIIFM, 1, 2, 4, 16, 20, 82, 83

WWH, 5, 13, 14